FOLKESTONE RAILWAYS

BY
BRIAN HART

WILD SWAN PUBLICATIONS

PREFACE

Fifty years ago a young mum used to wheel her two-year-old in his pushchair to Park Road in Cheriton. Clambering onto the low wall bordering the railway embankment, his tiny fingers would tightly grasp the blackened iron railings and here they would both wait for a train to pass. Expresses, locals, goods and boat trains all came steaming by as the Southern Region went about its regular daily business. He soon learned that the signal arms which bounced skywards heralded another train, prompting the plea 'Just one more' – and so it went on. The only way his exasperated mum might coax him away was the promise of a Bourbon biscuit from the row of glass-fronted tins bordering the counter of Leslie's provisions and grocery store in Cheriton High Street. How vivid are the memories which make those days seem like only yesterday.

When researching the history of railway development at Folkestone and its harbour, it soon became apparent that volumes could be written upon the subject. Nevertheless, it has long been my intention to write about some of the historical events which engendered the growth of Folkestone from humble beginnings to favoured and fashionable watering place of the Victorians and Edwardians. This era represented its zenith and yet none of this would have happened had it not been for the railway.

What follows is not meant to be an exhaustive account of the railway over the last 150 years. It is merely a glimpse, although uppermost in my mind has been the desire to convey something of the huge struggle to build the railway, most notably through to Dover. I am also mindful of the goodwill and effort of its townsfolk who were anxious to develop the wonderful seaside resort which finally emerged. Few towns presented such a rich mixture of thriving industry alongside such prestigious patronage by the titled and wealthy. Coupled with its favoured position and surrounding natural beauty, Folkestone remains historically fascinating. I feel obliged to apologize for my account tailing-off, following the demise of steam in 1961. Coinciding with the rationalisation of the industry, brought about by successive governments, the railway was robbed of almost everything I found of interest.

Being fortunate enough to be born in Folkestone in 1949, I have an enduring affection for the town and I have included some of my own impressions in the closing pages. I hope those concerned only with historical facts and figures (of which there are ample) might, therefore, forgive this minor indulgence. As a boy, I was indeed lucky to have the acquaintance of so many kind people. Councillor Eric Harrison wrote numerous articles about the town's railways and water-balance lifts in the early 1960s for the *Folkestone Gazette*, so I have him to thank for enthusing me. Similarly, having afternoon tea at Cecil Barnard's clifftop home 'Cliff Haven' on the Bayle, overlooking the harbour as steam-hauled trains departed, was an unforgettable treat. Norman Wakeman was also inspiring, as was his marvellous photographic collection which I found fascinating. However, perhaps no one encouraged my interest more in local history than Peter Davies, Reference Librarian at the Folkestone Library & Museum. Once he realized this pestering schoolboy was not wasting his time with so many questions, but genuinely interested, he could never do enough to help.

I hope this modest book might also serve as a little tribute to all those men, especially those who lost their lives, in the great struggle to build this wonderful railway for us. Their efforts endure whilst we, who glide so effortlessly in speed and comfort across Cubitt's mighty viaduct and along his stupendous railway through the Warren, surely remain in their debt.

Brian Hart
Uckfield

CHAPTER ONE
MARCHING ONWARD

OVER a hundred and fifty years ago a small fishing village of humble means and proportions bordered a stream which flowed down a lush green valley to a natural bay on the South Kent coast. The waves of the English Channel broke upon the shoreline where generations of men had put to sea in fishing boats to earn a living. Since the weather frequently prevented them from taking to their boats, income was often low and sporadic. Not surprisingly, some of them took to smuggling as a means of surviving hard times and, with the coast of France little more than twenty miles away, there were always those willing to risk gaol or the gallows.

Efforts to protect the meagre harbour were either minimal or non-existent during the early nineteenth century. Quite often the boats, cottages and sheds were at the mercy of severe storms which swept through the Straits of Dover. However, in summer this small settlement was extremely picturesque, its motley collection of ramshackle buildings, sail lofts, landing sheds, ale houses and dwellings of all shapes and sizes, cluttered about the valley bottom on either side of the Pent stream. Such was the appeal of the place that many artists and engravers frequently came to this spot. The most well-known was J. M. W. Turner, seemingly so anxious to capture its atmosphere that he deliberately sought out the company of the ordinary folk who went to sea 'mingling with humble and practical men'. Other visitors, it seems, were less captivated by this place where houses perched precariously upon hillsides along dark, narrow roads and alleyways. Few strangers to Folkestone were prepared to venture out after dusk when the only light was that from a candle or oil lantern, remaining instead within the safety of the few boarding establishments upon the West Cliff and around the parish church. Further westwards, the lonely, empty fields upon the cliff were given over to grazing cattle, yet within a few decades these same meadows would become one of the most fashionable and highly respectable areas for the exclusive enjoyment of the rich and aristocratic.

Upon the East Cliff the crumbling greensand hills rise to bolster the noble chalk range of the North Downs which meet the sea between Folkestone and Dover. Here, the secret wilderness of the Warren, a spot beloved by those with an interest in the natural sciences, stretches as far as the eye can see to Abbot's Cliff which juts imposingly and defiantly out to sea.

Behind the town, if its population of just 3,000 souls could justify such terminology, the valley created by the Pent stream millions of years ago led up to Bradstone Mill and on to the tiny hamlet of Foord. Situated in a pleasant rural setting was Foord Farm, close to the stream, whilst a fine and imposing residence known as Park House, owned by the Earl of Radnor, nestled not far away in a lush and enviable location. The surrounding pastures stretched north to the foot of the Downs and west towards other farmsteads and fine houses: Broad Mead, More Hall, Coolinge, Enbrook and Risborough. Shepherds of that era looked down upon open fields and the Pent valley towards the sea, the only sign of

mechanization being the rotating sails of windmills in the distance. However, this pastoral scene would start to disappear following the coming of the railway, which ultimately, for good or bad, changed the town forever and instigated the development of modern Folkestone.

There were numerous schemes for railways in Kent during those ambitious days of the 1820s and '30s. One envisaged railroads emanating from Canterbury like spokes on a cartwheel, whilst competitors were quick to realize the potential of building fast, straight lines to Dover and Folkestone. It was eventually left to the newly-formed South Eastern Railway which, in the summer of 1836, saw its grand designs approved by Parliament and given the Royal Assent. Brave and bold decisions were taken in the planning stages, most notably that of projecting the railway from Folkestone to Dover along the foot of the towering and precipitous cliffs bordering the English Channel.

From London the railway headed southwards to Red Hill where it would then diverge eastwards, running along the Vale of Kent to Tonbridge before passing through the small market town of Ashford and on to Folkestone. This route was based primarily on the whim of Parliament as a way of cutting costs and sharing with the London & Brighton Railway the difficulties in crossing the terrain of the North Downs, where expensive earthworks had to be incurred. Although this section demanded a long tunnel, the line eastwards from Red Hill to Folkestone was relatively simple whereby a fast, straight railway was anticipated. This is not to say that the new line could simply be laid more or less on the surface. Undulations in the land required the provision of further tunnels whilst, for most of its way, extensive embankments and cuttings were still necessary. However, there were no major obstacles until the route crossed the Foord valley behind Folkestone, then beyond into the Warren, with its unknown sub-strata. Its projection was indeed courageous since it would prove to be something of a surveyor's nightmare, yet with fortitude the railway was eventually driven through, an accomplishment which can only be described as an engineering triumph.

While the fields where the iron road was planned to run between Tonbridge and Folkestone were as yet undisturbed, the surveyors and engineers descended into the Warren with no delay, for it was here that the greatest challenges would be faced. Preliminary excavations for one of the two massive tunnels were already well under way during the spring of 1838. At the same time, test borings confirmed the surveyors' worst fears - that the whole mass of chalk rested upon beds of gault, a slippery bluish-grey clay. This area of Folkestone was popular with fossil hunters as the gault contains marvellous specimens of ammonites. It was also valuable to the brick-making industry and 'gaults', as they were known, provided very heavy, dense and durable bricks of a whitish colour. However, its presence was unwelcomed by those involved with the construction of railways. Rain penetrated the ground until it met the waterproof gault, thereby forming springs and spouts which made the chalk above unstable. The situation was further aggravated by the relentless action of the sea, which periodically caused huge landslides. Undaunted, however, the summer of 1839 saw navvies using the spoil from the twin bores beneath the impressive Shakespeare Cliff at Dover to elevate the railway back towards Folkestone and the next great obstacle, the Round Down headland. Not surprisingly, lives were soon lost once construction commenced, the first known being a man named Joseph Austen who perished in a sudden landslide, whilst four others were simultaneously crushed in the tunnelling beneath Shakespeare Cliff.

This important stage of the railway naturally created much interest and formed the focal point of the whole London to Dover line. The directors of the SER were frequently in Folkestone on official visits, whilst there was even more excitement when, on 15th August 1839, the *Kent Herald* reported:

> 'The *Fairless* steamer, with six Government Commissioners to survey the harbours on the South East Coast, came into this port on Tuesday at one o'clock. Another correspondent says: Her Majesty's steamship *Cornubia* arrived on Tuesday at Folkestone having on board Admiral Sir James Gordon, one of the Commissioners of Sheerness Dockyard, three or four Post Captains and two Government Engineers who inspected the Harbour as to its fitness for being made a place of refuge for ships of war and merchant vessels.
>
> Great preparations are in hand to commence the Railroad in this neighbourhood. The contractors and their company of workmen are now only waiting the arrival of barges upon the tide with their barrows and implements, which are hourly expected.'

Two months later it was revealed that the 'railroad' was progressing rapidly with over two hundred men working day and night in the vicinity of Folkestone. Fine weather during October enabled excavations in the Warren to proceed unhindered. It was an equally fortunate time for the townsfolk who had been 'on very short commons' in recent years. The Canterbury press commented on the many houses which had once stood empty, but were now all taken, adding: 'it is anticipated that Folkestone will again see a happy day'.

Outwardly, matters were progressing well. However, spiralling costs of the works through the Warren caused grave concern and astonishment when it was calculated that, at upwards of £60,000 per mile - a staggering amount at that time - the stretch between Folkestone and Dover would exceed expenditure on the entire preceding sixty miles. Nevertheless, progress remained rapid, whilst it was stated that the pace was faster in Folkestone than on any other part of the line.

Towards the end of 1839 the foundations were laid down for the 'skew arches' where the turnpike roads from Canterbury and Dover converged before descending into the town. Carts were used to carry beach and sand from the harbour, their constant comings and goings reported as making the town 'very lively'. Elsewhere, lime-burning pits were created to manufacture the huge amounts of mortar required by the armies of bricklayers.

Locals watched in amazement as engineering feats appeared to be accomplished with relative ease. Rails and wagons allowed gangs of three hundred men at a time to shift 54 tons of earth every hour over a distance of half a mile. This centred around the heading of the Martello tunnel which would enable entry into the Warren, the spoil being drawn back to build a massive embankment between the skew arches and the Foord valley.

Because construction was regulated by a series of contracts, there was no permanent security for the men who sweated and cursed as they hewed and heaved the soil. During May 1840 several of these contracts ceased on completion, with many men being laid-off. Since it was not known when fresh tenders would be issued, large numbers left the town in search of work elsewhere and without settling dues for their board and lodgings. It was reported that scarcely a person in the town who'd had dealings with the labourers had not suffered a financial loss as a result. Although wage levels are not given, it seems the navvies were not well paid for their toiling. Incidents of sheep and livestock stealing from nearby farms are recorded, whilst fourteen labourers were instantly dismissed during 1839 for pilfering timber.

With the arrival of spring in 1840 it was reported that a pair of sparrows had built their nest underneath the temporary wooden bridge at the skew arches. Despite the fact that wagons were trundling noisily overhead every few minutes to convey spoil, the plucky little birds steadfastly remained upon the eggs and successfully raised their fledglings, much to the pleasure of the workmen.

The treacherous nature of the land formation throughout the Warren, coupled with the hazards of railway building, inevitably led to further deaths. During July it was estimated that the line had claimed at least thirty lives either through instant death or injuries sustained during construction. In spite of these dreadful casualties, the pace of work was hastened, assisted in the main by a warm, dry summer. The people of Folkestone were in the habit of walking out to see the sites of interest and were full of admiration for the skill of the bricklayers who had recently been building the skew bridge, 'a beautiful construction of two oblique arches, a curiosity and well worthy of a visit'. The more venturesome wandered over the East Cliff and into the Warren to see the deep cutting, 'a work of art much to be admired'. However, the naturalists were unimpressed and felt that the iron road had irrevocably despoiled the once-secret and beloved treasure house of plants and insects by its unwelcome intrusion.

The lining of Shakespeare tunnel appears to have begun during 1840, but regretfully it was not without incident. At the end of October a boat laden with over 2,000 bricks struck a rock and quickly sank, drowning two men, although two boys who were dragged out of the sea thankfully recovered. Further deaths followed as the winter set in and we might well contemplate the sometimes appalling conditions in which these hardiest of men toiled. Most were used to 'roughing it', sleeping in bitterly cold shacks, or even barns if they could remain undetected. A young farm lad in the employ of Mr. Kingsnorth of Ingles Farm had an unpleasant fright one frosty morning when he went to fetch some straw and stumbled instead upon the corpse of a railway labourer beneath a hay stack. The coroner concluded that the man had simply perished in the cold.

Even though the weather continued to worsen, the prospects for working men improved with many fresh hands being taken on in January 1841. The embankments on either side of the Foord valley were nearing completion, whilst more praise was heaped upon the skew arches which 'present a beautiful appearance and form a noble and imposing entrance to the town'.

Excavations at Abbot's Cliff were meanwhile being 'pursued with activity' with mining navvies deep inside the huge cliff as the long cavern was hewn out of the chalk. Beyond here the sea wall towards Shakespeare Cliff was being constructed, 'a splendid piece of work, being of much credit to Mr. Bolcomb who, under the contractor, Mr. Lambert of Brighton, superintends the work'. Elsewhere, the formation of the railway to the west of Folkestone was simultaneously taking shape, while a start was made upon a short tunnel at Sandling, near Newing Green.

Generally speaking, it was a time of considerable optimism and good fortune since many hundreds of men were employed. Brickmakers, bricklayers, carpenters, blacksmiths, carters, labourers, as well as the numerous tradesmen in the town and suppliers of goods, enjoyed a boom which happily provided much in the way of means to families whom, only a few years before, had been on the breadline.

Another milestone was reached during the second week of May 1841 when the excavation at Shakespeare tunnel was finally completed and all the workmen enjoyed 'a grand treat' in celebration. It is probable that, as this great scheme gradually took shape, the directors and shareholders of the SER gained some considerable comfort as each major project was brought to a successful conclusion. It is also quite possible that no one really knew with any certainty whether the railway could be driven through such an unstable terrain or, moreover, guess as to how long it might remain intact. A disturbing foretaste of what was to come took place in the following November when heavy rains waterlogged the land, which resulted in some very heavy chalk falls between Shakespeare Cliff and another headland on the Folkestone side, the Round Down. Whereas Abbot's Cliff was sound enough for a single bore, Shakespeare Cliff, as mentioned earlier, necessitated twin bores with Gothic arches as the pointed arch is strongest of all. Initial tests conducted at Round Down proved it to be riddled with faults and confirmed suspicions that it was quite incapable of being tunnelled through. The alignment of the railway would also place a tunnel too close to the face of the cliff. While expert advice was sought for a solution, the undaunted directors were pleased to report at the end of 1841 that the Warren and Folkestone contracts had been completed to formation level, whilst arrangements were in hand for driving the tunnel at Saltwood, four miles west of the town. No doubt the SER board were gratified by the engineer's report which stated that the railway was expected to be opened as far as Tonbridge during May 1842 and to Staplehurst Road by midsummer, with Ashford being on the railway map by the end of the year.

Perhaps surprisingly, these predictions came true, since public trains began operating between Tonbridge and London from 26th May. Four trains ran each way on weekdays, with two on Sundays. A favourable testimonial appeared in a local paper which spoke of 'the extremely easy motion of the carriages and perfect regularity of the trains which has found great favour among all those who have ridden in them'.

While the railway was being forged ahead with such rapidity, the little harbour at Folkestone was not being neglected. Indeed, much had changed during the past few years which most likely displeased the fishermen. The once-sleepy bay had been transformed into a place of frantic activity and industry. Throughout the summer of 1842 the small quayside was crammed with all kinds of vessels, while others waited in the offing until there was room to unload. Barques and barges jostled for a space on every tide, replete with all kinds of materials used not only for railway building, but creating modern Folkestone. Quite often, fourteen brigs at a time crowded in among the fishing smacks as sloops and other vessels delivered cargoes of coals, ashes, timber, stone and iron. One contractor alone was reported to be regularly using a hundred tons of coal a week and bringing 'more hustle and bustle in our town than was ever known here'. Not surprisingly, the paving setts along the narrow streets were soon dislodged and torn up with the incessant wear and tear of heavy loads.

The cost of this section of the SER's system was still proving dauntingly expensive. Those who could read were no doubt astounded to pick up their newspapers to learn that the weekly bill to the SER in pursuing the works at Folkestone amounted to over £11,000. The local press considered this 'an almost incredible' sum of money. As each month passed by there came about a mounting sense of excitement, even though it would be yet another year before the first train might steam into Folkestone. From the high, windswept ridges of the North Downs a panoramic view was obtained of the great sweep of railway embankments and cutttings from Beachborough, through Cheriton Street and on to Folkestone. Looking down from Sugar Loaf Hill, above Park Farm, great mounds of chalk spoil could be seen looming skywards on either side of the once-rural Foord valley in readiness for the commencement of the viaduct. Horses and men were everywhere, the cobbled narrow lanes echoing to the clatter of hooves and iron-rimmed wheels of heavily-burdened carts, while at the harbour a constant sense of urgency and sometimes unregulated chaos existed from dawn till dusk.

On Tuesday 23rd August 1842 the first brick was ceremoniously laid at the commencement of lining out Abbot's Cliff tunnel. The workmen were 'regaled with refreshments' before the mammoth task of multi-lining the 1 mile 182-yards bore.

A week later it was revealed that the government had, at length, resolved to sell Folkestone harbour, whilst it was simultaneously reported that Messrs Grissell & Peto, railway contractors, had offered a large sum for it. Much of the beach, which had latterly prevented larger vessels from entering, had been removed as a result of the many craft taking it on as ballast following delivery of railway material. Ships which required from 18 to 20 feet draught were henceforth able to dock with ease. Nevertheless, the problems of silting had yet to be addressed.

During that same month four men had a fearful brush with death while working in the Martello tunnel. A sudden collapse of earth buried them alive, but thankfully they were within reach to be dug out. Less fortunate was another workman who, only days later, expired after being struck on the head by a dislodged chalk boulder which toppled down a ventilation shaft and fractured his skull.

On 31st August the SER was able to open Headcorn station on the other side of Ashford. Accordingly, a new stagecoach service was introduced at Dover to connect with London trains, This was initiated by Mr. Worthington of the Ship Hotel, but it wasn't long before other omnibuses were seen plying to and fro along the Ashford road to Headcorn.

Within the space of just four years Folkestone had changed almost beyond recognition, a fact not unnoticed as revealed in the *Kent Herald* of 22nd September 1842:

'We are "marching onward". The proposed introduction of gas light into our streets, houses and shops; the bustle occasioned by the landings of immense quantities of materials for the railway, and their transit to the line; the crowded state of the streets in the evening, from the great number of navvies and brickmakers employed on the works and other mechanics resident in the town, altogether have made so great a change in the place as to excite our wonder. In the meantime it is to be remarked that a desire of improvement has manifested itself as regards the adaptation of the town for better residences and improved throroughfares; and it is not unlikely but the next spring season may exhibit a new town arising, by an extension of the present one, upon the border of the rail-line.'

West of Folkestone the scene was one of equal activity as, encouraged by favourable weather, work continued day and night on the portion between Hythe (Westenhanger) and Ashford. Although the directors and engineers of the SER expressed their great satisfaction at the progress being made, the public seemed impatient. Hythe was 'quite choked up' with the private carriages of the nobility on their way to and from Headcorn station, while well-filled public conveyances ran daily to the temporary terminus.

Those who journeyed upon the rough roads at that time could see for themselves the rapid progress being made upon the railway. However, not everything went as smoothly as sometimes anticipated. Problems with excessive water, caused by powerful springs draining down from the chalk downs, led to delays between Cheriton and Sandling Park at Saltwood tunnel. The SER therefore called in 'a very formidable corps of miners' who were soon able to divert the flows into pipes for use elsewhere. As with most of the other major sites of engineering, an entire settlement was created in the green fields beside and above the tunnel. Following the opening of the line, the entire 'village' was sold off lock, stock and barrel. Over 1,000 items, including complete cottages, stores, weighhouses, stables, mangers, privvies, wagons, carts and surplus materials were sold at auction in July 1843 by Messrs. Finnis & Ronalds of Hythe.

Whilst it may be acknowledged that everyone admired the perseverance and hard work displayed by the miners and workmen employed by the railway contractors, there were many who resented this influx into the town. The frankly suspicious relationship between the navvies and the locals took a turn for the worse on the night of Monday 10th October 1842 when a large number, most of whom had been drinking heavily, began rioting in the streets. The few policemen were quite unable to control such a threat and sought assistance from Captain Peake and his men of the Coast Guard Service. The notorious Riot Act was read out to the noisy assembly, who only dispersed once three of the ringleaders had been arrested and taken away.

The approach of winter saw the completion of bricking Shakespeare Cliff tunnel when the highly-imposing inclined Gothic portals were cleared of scaffolding. Sadly, a young man lost his life only a few days beforehand when a loaded skiff of bricks being lowered down one of the ventilation shafts suddenly toppled and crushed him.

Although the dreadful toll in human lives continued, 1st December 1842 was a day for celebrations since it witnessed the opening of the line as far as Ashford. Benjamin Cubitt, a brother of William Cubitt, the chief engineer of the SER, climbed aboard a Sharp, Roberts 2-2-2 engine, No.20, named *Harold* and drove a party 'at a quick and even pace' to Headcorn and back.

With six months yet to go before a scheduled opening to Folkestone, pressure on the contractors intensified. Messrs. Grissell & Peto, who were due to complete Saltwood tunnel by June 1843, appear to have been under obligation to meet that date or risk incurring financial penalties. In fact, Saltwood was the last obstacle in the way of actually bringing the railway to the vicinity of Folkestone. However, the completion of the line to the authorized 'station house' which was in course of being built between the Foord valley and Martello tunnel depended upon the viaduct. A temporary station was therefore planned on the western, or Ashford, side of the valley. Some considerable excitement surrounded the building of the viaduct and its progress was eagerly followed in the local press. The *Kent Herald* spoke of the proposed structure which:

'...passes at the height of 100 feet above the surface of the mill stream and will consist of nineteen semi-circular arches of thirty feet space each, all of plain sound brickwork, without stone or expensive ornament of any kind; the foundations for all the piers and the abutments of this structure are in the course of execution and are nearly completed, the work is under contract to Messrs. Grissell & Peto. Messrs. Treadwell have completed the embankment from the viaduct and the cuttings in the Warren. Grissell & Peto expect to complete the Martello tunnel next spring. Mr. Wright, the resident engineer, progresses well with Abbot's Cliff tunnel.'

With the old year of 1842 coming to a close, the SER was able to feel confident about reaching the goal of Folkestone on schedule, followed soon after by the ultimate destination of Dover and thus securing its monopoly on the two most important channel ports. As for the people of Folkestone, this New Year was quite unlike any other since it heralded such great and profound changes. The mean and humble Folkestone of old would largely cease to exist following the opening of the railway. Already there were influential landowners and architects working in conjunction to create a great and gracious town which would rise from the meadows and fields surrounding this little settlement crowded around the Pent valley. As the first chime of midnight struck out the New Year of 1843 there could be no going back, whilst the realization of this exciting and tremendous achievement was barely months away.

CHAPTER TWO
RAILWAY TRIUMPH

AT the commencement of January 1843 plans were already in hand for solving the problem of Round Down. This huge promontory was described as being of a 'singularly bold and picturesque character' and, at a height of 375 feet, was even higher than Shakespeare Cliff. The SER's chief engineer, William Cubitt, came to the conclusion that the entire mass would have to be removed with dynamite. Needless to say, the prospect caused considerable excitement in Kent, whereby crowds of people gathered on the afternoon of Thursday, 26th January, to witness the occasion.

The calculations were thoroughly meticulous, being carefully implemented by the SER's miners to the most precise detail. Three separate 100-yard shafts were driven into the heart of the cliff, each leading to a chamber in which gunpowder was stacked in open boxes. 18,000 lbs of powder was equally distributed, with bursting charges being wired up to batteries. Cubitt reckoned that, on detonation, the gunpowder would have to shift 200,000 tons of chalk before its energy could find a vent. It was also thought possible that as much as a million tons would be dislodged.

At 9am a red flag was hoisted, whilst the area was roped off, with guards being posted at various points. An hour later William Cubitt arrived with other engineers and the directors for an inspection of Shakespeare and Abbot's Cliff tunnels before gazing, for the very last time, upon the Round Down which seemingly rose defiantly in between. Retiring to a marquee for refreshments, they watched the crowds arrive, while half a mile out to sea two steamships, both crammed with spectators, dropped anchor. At 2pm the atmosphere was described as 'intense and excitable as a quarter of an hour passed in deep anxiety'. Lieutenant Hutchinson of the Royal Engineers took up his position, ready to send the electrical charge along the wires which would heat up in the central chamber and cause the gunpowder to explode. On either side of him were two gentlemen who had the privilege of simultaneously detonating the other chambers. By this time the eyes and ears of the multitude were straining as hearts thumped in the almost unbearable tension of the moment. However, those anticipating a huge, roaring explosion, a spectacular bright flash and clouds of smoke accompanied by flying debris, were about to be hugely disappointed. At precisely 2.26pm the detonation was made. An eyewitness account in the *Kent Herald* described what happened next:

'A low, faint, indistinct and indescribable moaning was heard, and immediately afterwards the bottom of the cliff began to belly out, and then almost simultaneously about five hundred feet in breadth of the summit began gradually, but rapidly to sink, the earth on which the marquee was placed trembling sensibly under the shock. There was no roaring explosion, no bursting out of fire, no violent crashing and splintering of rocks, and comparatively speaking, very little smoke; for a proceeding of mighty and irresistible force, it had little or nothing of the

Sir William Cubitt, FRS, Civil Engineer, 1785-1861. From a drawing by J. H. Maguire 1850. CTY. PETER DAVIES

appearance of force and the rocks seemed to glide like a stream into the sea.'

The removal of Round Down in such a manner was undoubtedly one of many great triumphs in building this railway. However, the mass was not shifted in a single stroke and further minor detonations were necessary throughout the ensuing months before the formation of the line could be completed.

Apart from the recent excitement at Dover, there was equal interest in the works at Folkestone now that the huge viaduct was at last under construction. Even so, a horrifying mishap marred events when a young man in charge of the small steam engine which was used to pump water from the Pent stream out of the works, had his arm torn off by the flywheel. The constant threat of accidents must have been on every workman's mind, particularly when surgical treatment was so fearfully basic, and it is likely that serious injuries, or even deaths, were anticipated before the viaduct was finished. The *Kent Herald* kept its readers up to date with progress in the Foord valley and elsewhere:

'Folkestone: The works on the line between here and Saltwood are progressing rapidly and would well repay a visit. The viaduct near Folkestone is just emerging from the foundations, which appear to unite in them everything that skill and science can do to ensure their safety. The whole structure rises from a bed of concrete, laid in Roman cement. Between the piers (which when finished are to be about 80 feet high) are inverted arches, for the purposes, we suppose, of receiving any lateral pressure. They, as well as the piers, and, we believe, the whole viaduct, are to be laid in Roman cement.★ When finished, we think, it will be one of the most magnificent works on the whole line.'

During April the SER completed its purchase of Folkestone harbour for which it paid £18,000. The news was greeted with some satisfaction locally since this would ensure the future prosperity and development of the town. These thoughts were echoed in the local press which encouraged its readers to look to the future and not dwell instead upon the 'Folkestone of yore':

'We may predict from this most gratifying circumstance a great increase of prosperity to this long-neglected town, which, from the delightful scenery that surrounds it, its nearness to London, and shortness of communication with the continent, without doubt, entitles it to consideration.'

The great struggle to lay the foundations for modern Folkestone brought further deaths that month when, sadly, two more men were killed on site. George Tuggy, just 21 years of age, slipped with a barrow of bricks and tumbled down a ventilation shaft at the Martello tunnel. Only days later Daniel Higgins, a mining navvy, broke his back and eventually expired after falling eighty feet down Abbot's Cliff. Alas, it seemed the toll in human life would continue to be high.

On a happier note, there was much interest down at the harbour when new apparatus was installed for 'Kyanizing' the hundreds of wooden railway sleepers now arriving by ship on almost every tide. The process, patented in 1832, was named after its inventor, J. H. Kyan, whilst the 'receiver' enabled 144 sleepers at a time to be immersed for an hour in a corrosive solution, in this instance, per-chloride of mercury, to prevent decay. Around this time there was quite a variety of patented processes for preserving timber, many of which used unpleasant and often highly poisonous compounds of chemicals. 'Kyanizing', although found to be effective when properly applied, was expensive, whereby unless a full-strength solution was used the process failed. Not surprisingly, cheaper and more practical alternatives such as coal tar and creosote were eventually adopted by the railways. However, this business, as well as all the other daily activity, made the town extremely lively, whilst residents were kept informed of all the unfolding events:

'Mr. Morris is proceeding vigorously in his work of clearing the harbour - the tram waggons run over the east pier head and in a short time four hundred men will be employed, as the engagement is to have it cleared by September. It is the intention of the SER to make this a really fine and commodious haven - there will be 25 feet of water so that vessels of large tonnage may

★Roman cement was a highly caustic, lime-based product once used extensively for under-water work, but has now been superseded by Portland cement which possesses greater strength.

be able to enter with the greatest safety; the horn from the west pier head is to be carried out 200 feet into the sea, so fast steam boats can land or embark passengers at any time of the tide. Mr. Cubitt, the Company's Engineer, has taken lodgings here to superintend the works. The station houses and engine house [at what later became Folkestone Junction] are about half finished; a tram road and carriage road are set out, and property bought to construct the road from the station to the harbour, a distance of half a mile; the road is to come from the station house joining the Dover and Canterbury roads, through Mr. Holman's Pleasure Grounds, down Hague's Yard, through the Apollo Rooms, on to the harbour; a great many houses will come down.'

By the beginning of June, with only a matter of weeks before the planned opening of the line, the railway was in good shape, although there was still much to be done. Saltwood tunnel had been completed during the last week of May, whilst the engine shed and station buildings at Folkestone, (between Martello tunnel and the viaduct) were also finished. However, the railway could not be opened to this point until work on Foord viaduct had been concluded. Contemporary reports speak of a single line of rail being laid down for the purpose of an inspection by the SER directors as far as Coolinge (Shorncliffe) on Whit Monday, whilst a temporary station was in course of construction on the western side of the Foord valley. General Pasley, who inspected the line, commented that this makeshift station 'constructed of wood and canvas' would be pulled down as soon as the viaduct was finished. He was obviously much impressed by the standard of work achieved by the contractors which he concluded to be 'highly creditable'.

Attention was, of course, directed towards the harbour where the SER had recently purchased a boat building shop and land belonging to a Mr. Farley. Carpenters were employed to convert the building into a temporary inn until such time as work could begin on the construction of a large hotel on the site.

The wonderful opportunities which would come about with the opening of the railway to Folkestone seemed scarcely believable. The Kentish papers enthused about the prospect, even though opinion was tainted with the familiar xenophobia of the British press:

'If someone had once told you that soon, you may rise from your bed in London, breakfast on the seashore in England, partake of luncheon in Boulogne, spend a few hours there and have a good laugh at the Napoleon monument and yet that you should be back in London for dinner, why, you would set him down as a Bedlamite, or the projector of some joint stock Aerial Ship Company!'

The remaining days of June seemed to pass by quickly as efforts were made to complete the line as far as the temporary station near Foord viaduct. Finally, Saturday, 24th June dawned as the day when the first official train from London to Folkestone would run. Shortly before six o'clock there was much activity at London Bridge station as an entourage of SER directors and guests filed into the special train which was waiting to take them via Croydon, Red Hill

A rare, early sketch of 1843, depicting the temporary station at Folkestone on the embankment leading towards Foord valley.
COLLECTION ALAN TAYLOR

and Tonbridge to their long-awaited goal on the Kent coast. The 82-mile journey was completed in two hours and forty minutes, having stopped at five stations along the way. There was much cheering as Benjamin Cubitt, again at the controls of engine No.20 *Harold*, drove the train into the temporary terminus on the western hill above the Foord valley. Among those on board were Joseph Baxendale, the chairman of the SER, Mr. Lewis Cubitt and Decimus Burton, both noted architects, and, of course, William Cubitt whose engineering skills had been sorely tested to the limit in the creation of this grand railway. Carriages conveyed them to the harbour where the steamship *Water Witch* nudged the quayside. Their reception was enthusiastic in the extreme with loud cheering and clapping, whilst flags and bunting flew in the gentle wind of a perfect summer's day. The departure at 9.20am was equally celebratory as *Water Witch* swung away from the harbour before steaming out across the gentle swell to France. Fortunately the weather was calm so hardly anyone suffered the 'green and yellow melancholy' caused through being 'tossed about in Neptune's blanket'. At 12.30pm all passengers were landed safely whilst Boulogne went 'frantic' with excitement as the English visitors were warmly greeted by the amiable townsfolk. The English and French national airs were played with gusto by the bands, whereupon everyone received an extremely cordial welcome. In typical manner, 'toasts, viands and wines of the most costly description' generously came forth freely, whilst the 'arrangements in the style of elegance and taste for which the

French people are truly remarkable' were genuinely appreciated by the English guests. A most emotional farewell took place as *Water Witch* left Boulogne and headed back towards Folkestone, docking there at 6.30pm. Horse-drawn carriages waiting at the harbour then took the guests through the town and back to the temporary station. At five past seven the special train pulled out of Folkestone, arriving back at London Bridge three hours later, having called at eight stations en route.

During the following week, on Wednesday, 28th June 1843, the railway was opened to Folkestone for general traffic. Happily, it coincided with the Bayle Fair and the sixth anniversary of Her Majesty, Queen Victoria's coronation. The bells of the local churches were rung out across the town, whilst everywhere was festively decorated as people danced to music played by the bands. An even greater turnout was seen than on the previous Saturday as crowds flocked into the streets leading up to the railway where the 'neat and substantial' temporary station was 'thronged with spectators watching the movements of the various trains as they came and went'. The first train from London Bridge had arrived at 10.30am, amidst much cheering. From here, conveyances were in waiting for those who wished to carry on to Dover and the steam packets bound for the continent. Much interest was shown in the 'stupendous' viaduct, almost the last feat to be achieved before the railway reached Dover. However, work on the timber trestle viaduct above the beach on the Dover side of Shakespeare Cliff had only just commenced.

Sir William Cubitt's viaduct photographed in 1865. By this time the rural hamlet of Foord was already being developed as part of an expanding Folkestone as witnessed by the houses of 'Mount Pleasant' on the hillside.

COLLECTION PETER BAMFORD

With all the fuss and pomp surrounding the opening and subsequent attention upon Folkestone, it wasn't surprising that neighbouring Hythe, at one time a town of greater importance, should feel left out. Deputations were subsequently forthcoming during that summer for a station between Folkestone and Ashford to serve the town which, perhaps understandably, felt somewhat aggrieved. These were met with favour, whereby instructions were issued to prepare a site for a new station where Stone Street, the old Roman road from Hythe to Canterbury, crosses the railway.

During the ensuing months the branch line to the harbour was steadily pursued. On Wednesday, 8th September, workmen began pulling down many old properties along the route of the proposed line, whilst a number of trees on Mr. Holman's land went to the axe. In the meantime it was stated that the centring for three of the arches of the Foord viaduct had been fixed so that bricklayers were expected soon to begin work. A week later the *Kent Herald* revealed that gangs of men had descended upon the railway to the harbour where twenty houses had already been swept away with many more yet to go. By the end of the month eight arches of Foord viaduct were bricked in, whilst a start had been made in building the new harbour house and fine clock tower adjacent to the quaysides. Elsewhere, Martello tunnel had been finished, with the rails for the up line already laid and waiting to be connected on completion of the viaduct. Further works on the harbour involved the foundations for taking the railway upon twenty-one brick arches which formed a jetty and temporary embarkation pier.

The opening of the railway through to Folkestone station was scheduled for the late autumn, but a serious slip occurred in the huge embankment leading from there to the viaduct. This particular section proved troublesome in the years to come and, as my father recalls, even during the 1930s some portions were slipping and creeping into gardens of houses below. Foord viaduct was completed on Monday, 20th November, whereby on the following morning a locomotive and tender was despatched across the magnificent span for the first time. Not unexpectedly, there was some rejoicing; the structure gaily ornamented with flags, whilst all the workmen were treated to pints of ale. Happily, and perhaps remarkably, a local correspondent was able to pen: 'It must be gratifying to the feelings of the contractors Messrs. Grissell & Peto that this stupendous work has arrived at completion without appearance of settling at any point and without loss of life'. It is indeed remarkable that not a single life was sacrificed in the construction of Foord viaduct in view of the methods of working at that time. Railway construction was notoriously difficult, dangerous and arduous labour, where wooden scaffolding was lashed together with hemp rope, planks were placed precariously across giddy heights, whilst heavy loads of bricks and mortar had to be hoisted for turning these arches in the sky. The viaduct measured precisely 252 yards and six inches in length, comprising nineteen arches, with equal spans of 30 feet, whilst the highest point was above Bradstone Lane, at approximately 88 feet to rail level. The gleaming new brickwork of the structure crossing this rural valley was certainly a marvel to behold and completely changed the appearance of the tiny hamlet of Foord with its green pastures, millpond and meandering stream.

Three weeks later, on Tuesday, 12th December, the viaduct came to life when experimental trains were to be seen running over the graceful, slender arches and along the new line towards the Martello tunnel. Further progress was simultaneously being made with the 'tram-way' to the harbour, which it was hoped would be opened on New Year's Day, as well as the parallel carriage road from the station to the new Pavilion Hotel.

The SER's Board of Directors decided it would be appropriate to take a trip to Folkestone. Accordingly, on the afternoon of Thursday, 14th December, their special train could be seen crossing Cubitt's viaduct high above the valley. Finally, on Monday 18th, the temporary buildings and platforms west of the viaduct were closed and subsequently dismantled, whilst the new station, simply called 'Folkestone', opened to the public. Although the elegance of the viaduct

Handbill on the opening of the railway to Folkestone.
COLLECTION PETER BAMFORD

LONDON AND DOVER RAILWAY,

OPEN TO FOLKESTONE, SEVEN MILES FROM DOVER.

DOWN TRAINS

Distances.	DOWN TRAINS	Daily Trains (except Sundays): 8 A. M. Fast. 1, 2 Class	9¼ A.M. 1, 2, 3 Class	11½ A. M. Fast. 1, 2 Class	1½ P. M. 1, 2, 3 Class	4 P. M. 1, 2 Class	5¼ P.M. 1, 2, 3 Class	8½ P.M. Fast. 1, 2 Class	12 P.M. Goods only.	Sunday Trains: 7½ A.M. 1, 2, 3 Class	9¼ A.M. 1, 2, 3 Class	1½ P.M. 1, 2, 3 Class	4 P.M. 1, 2, 3 Class	8½ P.M. 1, 2, 3 Class
Miles		h.m.	h.m.	h.m.	h.m.	h.m.	h.m.	h.m.	h.m.	h.m.	h.m.	h.m.	h.m.	h.m.
0	London	8. 0	9.30	11.30	1.30	4. 0	5.30	8.30	12. 0	7.30	9.30	1 30	4 0	8,30
3	New Cross	8,13	9.44	11.43	1.44	4.14	5.44	8.43	12.24	7.44	9.44	1.44	4 14	8.44
10½	Croydon	....	10. 4	....	2. 4	4.34	6. 4	....	12.47	8. 4	10. 4	2. 4	4 34	9. 4
21	Reigate	8.55	10.32	12.25	2.32	5. 2	6.32	9.25	1.20	8.32	10.32	2.32	5. 2	9.32
26	Godstone	....	10.46	....	2.46	5.16	6.46	....	1.37	8.40	10.46	2.46	5.16	9.46
31	Edenbridge	....	11. 0	....	3. 0	5.30	7. 0	9.49	1.54	9. 0	11. 0	3. 0	5.30	10. 0
36	Penshurst	....	11.13	....	3.13	5.43	7.13	....	2.10	9.13	11.13	3.13	5.43	10.13
41	Tunbridge	9.37	11.25	1. 7	3.25	5.55	7.25	10.10	2.30	9.25	11.25	3.25	5.55	10.25
46	Maidstone Rd.	9.52	11.41	1.22	3.41	6.11	7.41	10.25	2.53	9.41	11.41	3 41	6.11	10.41
50	Marden	....	11.54	....	3.54	....	7.54	....	3. 9	9.54	11.54	3.54	6.24	10.54
53	Staplehurst	10. 8	12. 3	1.38	4. 3	6.30	8. 3	10.41	3.19	10.10	12. 3	4. 3	6.33	11. 3
56	Headcorn	....	12.12	....	4.12	....	8.12	....	3.31	10. 3	12.12	4.12	6.42	11.12
61	Pluckley	....	12.26	....	4.26	6.50	8.26	....	3.48	10.26	12.26	4.26	6.56	11.26
67	Ashford	10.40	12.42	2.10	4.42	7. 6	8.42	11.13	4. 6	10.42	12.42	4.42	7.12	11.42
82	Folkestone	11.13	1.17	2.43	5.17	7.41	9.17	11.46	4.54	11.17	1.17	5.17	7.47	12.17

DOWN TRAINS	Fares from London: Passengers 1st Class	Passengers 2nd Class	Carriages 2 wh.	Carriages 4 wh.	Horses 1 h.	Horses (if one property) 2 h.	Horses (if one property) 3 h.	Fares from New Cross: Passengers 1st Class	Passengers 2nd Class	Passengers 3rd Class	Carriages 2 wh.	Carriages 4 wh.	Horses 1 h.	Horses (if one property) 2 h.	Horses (if one property) 3 h.
	s. d.	s. d.	s.	s. d.	s.	s.	s.	s. d.	s. d.	s. d.	s. d.	s. d.	s.	s.	s.
London	....	....	..	....	..	..	..	....	....	....	....	....	..	..	..
New Cross	....	....	..	....	..	..	..	....	....	....	....	....	..	..	..
Croydon	2 3	1 9	6	8 0	7	10	15	1 6	1 2	1 0	5 0	7 0	6	9	14
Reigate	4 8	3 4	8	10 6	9	16	22	4 0	2 6	1 6	6 6	9 0	8	15	21
Godstone	5 4	3 8	10	13 0	12	18	24	4 6	3 0	1 8	7 6	11 6	10	16	22
Edenbridge	5 6	4 0	10	15 0	15	20	30	4 8	3 4	1 10	8 6	13 6	12	18	27
Penshurst	6 6	4 6	10	15 0	15	20	30	5 6	3 8	2 0	8 6	13 6	12	18	27
Tunbridge	7 6	5 0	10	15 0	15	20	30	6 0	4 0	2 6	8 6	13 6	12	18	27
Maidstone Rd.	7 6	5 0	10	15 0	15	20	30	6 0	4 0	2 6	8 6	13 6	12	18	27
Marden	8 0	5 6	..	....	..	..	..	6 6	4 6	2 9	....	....	..	..	..
Staplehurst	9 0	6 0	14	21 0	18	24	36	7 6	5 0	3 4	12 0	18 0	16	22	32
Headcorn	10 0	7 0	17	26 0	22	38	42	8 6	6 0	3 8	15 0	24 0	20	36	40
Pluckley	11 6	7 6	21	31 0	24	40	52	10 0	6 6	4 0	19 0	29 0	22	38	50
Ashford	13 6	8 6	25	35 0	28	44	56	12 0	7 6	4 6	23 0	33 0	26	42	54
Folkestone	17 0	11 0	40	55 0	40	60	80	15 6	10 0	6 0	38 0	53 0	38	58	78

☞ Powerful and well-appointed Steamers—the Emerald and Sir William Wallace—run with every tide between Folkestone and Boulogne, performing the passage either way in the short period of three hours. Saloon, 8s.; Chief Cabin, 6s.; Children under 10 years of age half-price; Carriages, 4 wheels, £2; do. 2 wheels, £1; Horses, £1; Dogs, 3s. From Dover, commodious Packets for Calais, Boulogne, Ostend, and other Ports, are constantly departing. At Folkestone the South Eastern Pavilion will afford the traveller every desirable accommodation at a reasonable rate.

UP TRAINS

Distances.	UP TRAINS	Daily Trains (except Sundays): 6.5 A. M. 1, 2, 3 Class	7.10 A. M. 1, 2 Class	9.50 A. M. Fast. 1, 2 Class	11.40 A. M. 1, 2, 3 Class	3.5 P. M. Fast. 1, 2 Class	6.35 P. M. 1, 2, 3 Class	8.25 P. M. 1, 2 Class	11.5 P. M. Goods only.	Sunday Trains: 6.50 A. M. 1, 2, 3 Class	9.50 A. M. 1, 2, 3 Class	12.50 P. M. 1, 2, 3 Class	3 50 P. M. 1, 2, 3 Class	6.50 P.M. 1, 2, 3 Class
Miles		h. m.	h. m.	h. m.	h. m.	h. m.	h. m.	h. m.	h. m.	h. m	h. m.	h. m.	h. m.	h. m.
0	Folkestone	6. 5	7.10	9.50	11.40	3. 5	6.35	8.25	11. 5	6.50	9.50	12.50	3.50	6.50
15	Ashford	6.45	7.50	10.30	12.20	3.45	7.15	9. 5	11.55	7.30	10.30	1.30	4.30	7.30
21	Pluckley	6.58	8. 3	....	12.33	....	7.28	9.18	12.10	7.43	10.43	1.43	4.43	7.43
26	Headcorn	7.11	....	....	12.46	....	7.41	....	12.25	7.56	10.56	1.56	4.56	7.56
29	Staplehurst	7.20	8.23	11. 0	12.55	4.15	7.50	9.38	12.39	8. 5	11. 5	2. 5	5. 5	8. 5
32	Marden	7.29	....	....	1. 4	....	7.59	....	12.50	8.14	11.14	2.14	5.14	8.14
36	Maidstone Rd.	7.42	8.41	11.15	1.17	4 30	8.12	9.56	1. 6	8.27	11.27	2.27	5.27	8.27
41	Tunbridge	8. 0	8.59	11.33	1.35	4 48	8.30	10.14	1.32	8.45	11.45	2.45	5.45	8.45
46	Penshurst	8.10	9. 9	....	1.45	....	8.40	10.24	1.44	8,55	11.55	2.55	5.55	8,55
51	Edenbridge	8.24	9.23	....	1.59	....	8.54	10.38	2. 0	9. 9	12. 9	3. 9	6. 9	9. 9
56	Godstone	8.38	9.37	....	2.13	....	9. 8	10.52	2.16	9.23	12.23	3.23	6.23	9.23
61	Reigate	8.52	9.51	12.15	2.27	5.30	9.22	11. 6	2.34	9.37	12.37	3.37	6.37	9.37
71½	Croydon	9.17	10.16	....	2.52	....	9.47	11.31	3. 2	10. 2	1. 2	4. 2	7. 2	10. 2
79	New Cross	9.35	10.34	12.53	3.10	6. 8	10. 5	11.49	3.25	10.20	1.20	4.20	7.20	10.20
82	London	9.45	10.44	1. 3	3.20	6.18	10.15	11.59	3.35	10.30	1.30	4.30	7.30	10.30

UP TRAINS	Fares to London: Passengers 1st Class	Passengers 2nd Class	Carriages 2 wh.	Carriages 4 wh.	Horses 1 h.	Horses (if one property) 2 h.	Horses (if one property) 3 h.	Fares to New Cross: Passengers 1st Class	Passengers 2nd Class	Passengers 3rd Class	Carriages 2 wh.	Carriages 4 wh.	Horses 1 h.	Horses (if one property) 2 h.	Horses (if one property) 3 h.
	s. d.	s. d.	s.	s. d.	s.	s.	s.	s. d.	s. d.	s. d.	s. d.	s. d.	s.	s.	s.
Folkestone	17 0	11 0	40	55 0	40	60	80	15 6	10 0	6 0	38 0	53 0	38	58	78
Ashford	13 6	8 6	25	35 0	28	44	56	12 0	7 6	4 6	23 0	33 0	26	42	54
Pluckley	11 6	7 6	21	31 0	24	40	52	10 0	6 6	4 0	19 0	29 0	22	38	50
Headcorn	10 0	7 0	17	26 0	22	38	42	8 6	6 0	3 8	15 0	24 0	20	36	40
Staplehurst	9 0	6 0	14	21 0	18	24	36	7 6	5 0	3 4	12 0	18 0	16	22	32
Marden	8 0	5 6	..	....	..	..	..	6 6	4 6	2 9	....	....	..	..	..
Maidstone Rd.	7 6	5 0	10	15 0	15	20	30	6 0	4 0	2 6	8 6	13 6	12	18	27
Tunbridge	7 6	5 0	10	15 0	15	20	30	6 0	4 0	2 6	8 6	13 6	12	18	27
Penshurst	6 6	4 6	10	15 0	15	20	30	5 6	3 8	2 0	8 6	13 6	12	18	27
Edenbridge	5 6	4 0	10	15 0	15	20	30	4 8	3 4	1 10	8 6	13 6	12	18	27
Godstone	5 4	3 8	10	13 0	12	18	24	4 6	3 0	1 8	7 6	11 6	10	16	22
Reigate	4 8	3 4	8	10 6	9	16	22	4 0	2 6	1 6	6 6	9 0	8	15	21
Croydon	2 3	1 9	6	8 0	7	10	15	1 6	1 2	1 0	5 0	7 0	6	9	14
New Cross	....	....	..	....	..	..	..	....	....	....	....	....	..	..	..
London	....	....	..	....	..	..	..	....	....	....	....	....	..	..	..

The timetable printed on the reverse of the handbill shown on the previous page.

COLLECTION PETER BAMFORD

One of the best early views of Folkestone (Junction) station, taken around 1890, looking towards Dover. Although the negative has been retouched, there is a wealth of interesting detail. Staggered platforms were favoured by the SER, although the Board of Trade disapproved of passengers having to risk their lives on the boarded crossings, whereby footbridges were later provided.

could not be appreciated from a railway carriage, the experience of riding high above the valley in one of the SER's open 3rd class carriages on a windy day must have been memorable to say the least. Anyone of a nervous disposition, as well as those who were obliged to hold firmly on to bowler hats and bonnets, could be forgiven any feelings of trepidation with nothing but a perilous drop barely a few feet away.

In spite of the fact that passengers had to detrain here and transfer to horse-drawn conveyances for the journey to the harbour, the popularity of the route seems to have far exceeded expectations. In the short space of five months it was stated that over 20,000 people had used the Folkestone-Boulogne route which commenced operating on 2nd August. For the time being the harbour branch was destined to be used only for goods traffic, but already it was hoped to run passenger trains into a station situated on the quayside.

The first train to run down the 'tram road' left Folkestone station on the morning of Tuesday, 16th January 1844, running as far as the 'Victoria' public house in South Street, before returning 'with a great number of persons' - presumably workmen. It was possible to make up for recent delays, caused by bad weather, through taking on extra hands. As well as the rush to complete the branch railway, the harbour itself was a scene of great activity where stones and mud were being cleared out. Unfortunately, this led to an increase in the size of the shingle bank at the mouth of the harbour which in turn obstructed vessels. The SER looked to creating a backwater, similar to that employed at Whitstable where tidal water could be trapped and used to flush out accumulated silt at ebb tide. Another method under consideration was the stopping-up of the Pent stream; however, there was insufficiency in its volume. Even though neither scheme was pursued, the SER did in fact go as far as

issuing demolition notices to the occupants of five hundred properties in the locality!

Visible signs of the popular Folkestone that was to come began with the opening of the South Eastern Railway's Pavilion Hotel, whilst close by a handsome harbour house was nearing completion, its clock tower with four illuminated faces being quite a talking point. Folkestone station was described as 'commodious in every way', whilst horse-drawn carriages waited upon every train to convey passengers to the harbour, or Dover, Sandgate and Hythe. Steam boats arrived and departed with every tide, whilst the road from the station to the harbour was quite a marvel since it was illuminated along the whole of its length with gas. For the first time the streets of Folkestone were described as being regularly swept, well-lit and much improved. Indeed, the old fishing hamlet had changed almost beyond recognition now that the railway had finally arrived. Attention to the needs of Hythe had not been overlooked, for already the SER had laid out a station a mile to the west of Sandling Park - so far the only intermediate stop between Ashford and Folkestone. This new station was called 'Westenhanger for Hythe', although its public opening was delayed until trains were running through to Dover.

At long last this great feat of early Victorian engineering was finished. It was a marvel of its time and due largely to the genius of William Cubitt whose courage and fortitude had finally won him the respect and admiration he undoubtedly deserved. Many saw it as a triumph over the forces of nature, the wilderness tamed to serve the needs of progress and commerce, whilst others, with perhaps good reason, regretted the disturbance and partial loss of so much natural beauty. In spite of this, the 7th February 1844 was a day reserved for celebration and looking firmly to the future as the first public train left Folkestone for Dover.

One of the earliest photographs of the harbour taken around 1856, showing three paddle-steamers moored alongside the South Quay at low tide. The SER workshops in the foreground had rail connections to the harbour branch by way of small wagon turntables along the Stade.
COLLECTION ALAN TAYLOR

CHAPTER THREE
VICTORIAN PROGRESS

WHEREAS the planned opening of the railway line through the Warren to Dover was not delayed by the contractor's workmen, the British weather almost brought proceedings to a standstill. During the first week of February heavy falls of snow carpeted the Kentish landscape, completely blocking the new railway between Folkestone and Ashford. Throughout Friday, 2nd February 1844, trains were seriously delayed with passengers on board having a bitterly cold and frustrating time. The 9.30am from Folkestone did not reach London Bridge until six o'clock in the evening, whilst the 8am from London eventually pulled into Folkestone at half past five. A contemporary account in the local paper provides a useful insight into the working of SER trains at this time by revealing that this latter train 'was accompanied by the intermediate trains, making up in the whole, about thirty carriages, propelled by five engines'. The goods services fared no better either, the midnight departure from London taking nine and a half hours to get through due to the deep snow drifts near Westenhanger.

Within a week or two, so it appears, the snow had melted away and life returned to normal. Westenhanger station was opened and, by all accounts, was being well-used since numerous omnibuses were seen plying to and from Hythe. Visitors were evidently finding it easy to travel as the local paper commented that they were flooding into the town, adding:

> 'It has been said that Folkestone is the only place in England which has benefited by a railway passing it and we venture to predict that the permanent benefit arising to the town is only just beginning to be felt and is not yet half appreciated. All its houses have marvellously risen in value and are occupied. Landlords have been able to treble their rents compared to three years ago and trade, which was once at such a low ebb, has now increased wonderfully.'

The harbour branch was likewise opened at this time, but for goods traffic only. A Folkestone correspondent reported at the beginning of March that the first cargo of coals had been taken up the 'tramway' with the locomotive hauling about twelve tons on each trip to the 'upper' (Junction) station where it was then despatched to other destinations. With the branch line and harbour now fully operational, the engine shed at Folkestone housed a number of locomotives which were 'kept in readiness night and day'.

The first of a number of accidents on the harbour branch took place only weeks after it was brought into use when a labourer named Gilbert was killed. Apparently two empty wagons descended the incline, which for much of its length falls at 1 in 30, only to collide with another which ran over the unfortunate workman. Gilbert had been engaged on the new cart road being laid down so that domestic fuel could be delivered around the town. As well as coal, it was stated that quantities of corn and oilcake were also coming in during that week.

A notable occasion, and only the first of many, was the arrival of the Royal Train on Thursday 28th March on its way through to Dover. The train, which completed the journey from London in just over two hours, conveyed Prince Albert who was on his way to visit his native Germany. The *Kent Herald* remarked that the compartment, in the marvellous railway carriage provided by the SER for the exclusive use of Victoria and Albert, was lined throughout with pure white satin.

Travelling by train was not quite so comfortable for ordinary folk. During April a new iron steamship *Orion* was brought into service on the Folkestone-Boulogne route. Not surprisingly, this engendered a rise in the number of people who were keen to make their first trip to France and back in a day. In fact, the railway was becoming far too popular and barely able to cope with demand. A Sunday excursion at the end of May was described as being so crammed that there was scarcely standing room. The train, which started out from the SER's London terminus at Bricklayers Arms, comprised forty carriages containing almost 2,000 people and was 'impelled by four engines'. Presumably some of these were dropped off on the way for other destinations since, on arrival at Folkestone, only two engines were being used to haul 26 carriages.

Railway travel was evidently much in favour, but not everyone enjoyed the new experience. In July, an evening train became held up in a tunnel in the Warren for about twenty minutes, causing great consternation among the passengers who were surrounded by total darkness. It was stated that this had 'been the case three or four times lately'. There were also delays caused by locomotive failures. The last train for London one Wednesday evening 'met with an impediment near the Cheriton Mill [Risborough Lane] from the breaking of the pedestal of the engine'. It took half an hour before the train could proceed, during which time a spare locomotive was 'procured from Coolinge' which seems to suggest that in 1844 there were at least sidings in the vicinity of what later became Shorncliffe station. Fires were another hazard and several are referred to, although no specific details are revealed. However, a new fire engine 'constructed upon a first rate principle' was henceforth kept under the arches of the harbour branch. In view of the fact that most of the buildings in the vicinity were constructed of tarred wood and that locomotives sent out showers of sparks on the run up the branch, it is truly remarkable that Folkestone didn't suffer some dreadful conflagration.

With fine weather during August, all the excursion trains were very heavily loaded. The last evening train returning to London from Folkestone comprised forty carriages which required 'propelling by four engines'. What a sight it must have made as the locomotives blasted their way across Foord viaduct – it is a pity that such a spectacle may only be conjured up in the imagination. Another returning excursion, this time hauled by three engines, evidently had insufficient power since it had to be divided with each portion being sent off with three engines apiece. Locomotive development was still, of course, very much in its infancy and from these accounts it may be judged how the ratio of steam power to the load requiring moving had yet to be properly assessed. Further evidence of this is revealed in an account of how a goods train from Dover to Folkestone came to grief in Shakespeare tunnel. Only one engine was attached to a large number of wagons, with the result that 'in striving to get on', one of its boiler tubes burst. Spare engines from Dover and Folkestone were therefore sent out to assist.

Even though the railway was fully operational there was still a great deal of work being carried out at various sites. Limekilns in the Warren were at full production and it was here that a young lad met with an untimely death when he was crushed between wagon buffers during September. Another fatality that month involved a workman who was killed when he fell off a 'jimmy' - a platelayers' trolley - and broke his neck. However, by far the worst accident around this period took place near the site of Round Down where work was still being carried out near the sea wall. Thirteen employees of Messrs. Grissell & Peto had put down their tools at midday for a meal break and, due to the driving rain, decided to force open a door leading into the cliff to find some shelter. The door had purposely been kept locked since it was used to store gunpowder, but no one apparently noticed this. One of the men then lit his pipe and carelessly threw down the match which immediately ignited surplus powder on the floor, causing a tremendous explosion. The carnage was quite appalling as they were all blown out of the cavern, some onto the cliff and others out to sea. Parts of their remains were later washed up on the beach, whilst other bodies were scattered about the railway.

Accidents such as these were always regrettable; however, there was considerable outrage when a deliberate attempt was made in November 1844 to derail a train near the Cheriton arch. A London-bound service from Dover, double-headed, with 150 passengers on board, left Folkestone when, minutes later, it struck a number of planks where the line crosses Cheriton Road. Fortunately, a guard on the first carriage spotted the obstruction and was able to signal to the two other guards to apply their brakes. The dozen wooden planks were crushed by the leading engine's wheels, but happily it was not derailed and the train was saved from being dragged down the 50ft-high embankment. Whoever was responsible for committing such a malevolent act remained a mystery, but the local paper commented upon the fact that a 'beer shop' was situated a short distance away where 'a number of loose characters were found upon whom suspicion fell'. However, the landlord and his patrons protestingly disclaimed all knowledge of the affair.

The development of modern Folkestone relied for the most part on the establishment of the railway and subsequent continental links. Large parts of the town and the surrounding area were owned by the influential Radnor family and in 1845 a prospectus was issued which detailed plans for its transformation, whilst the noted London architect Sidney Smirke was engaged to design the estate. Smirke came up with grandiose plans for both the West Cliff and Wear Bay estates, the latter stretching from the harbour, over the East Cliff and as far as the Warren. To link these prestigious developments, which envisaged tree-lined avenues, handsome villas, gracious squares and meticulously-planned gardens, an imposing railway bridge was constructed across the harbour branch. East Cliff bridge was finished in the New Year of 1845, at a cost of over £10,000 which was paid for by Lord Radnor. However, this elegant three-arch brick structure was destined to see very little of the fine carriage and landau traffic of the well-heeled as had been hoped. Smirke's plans for the East Cliff were never taken up, leaving only the West Cliff to enjoy the eventual patronage of wealthy and titled visitors. Nevertheless, there was no doubt in 1845 that Folkestone and its inhabitants, from all walks of life, owed much to the coming of the railway:

'A marvellous change has been wrought in the circumstance of this town by the South Eastern Railway. If any place on the coast of England is entitled to a visit or to be patronised as a watering place, it is Folkestone. Although the town, at present, offers but little attraction, it will, probably, at no distant period be raised not only to be one of the most important towns on the south coast of England, but also to be a favourite watering place.'

Perhaps the arrival of the railway was something of a double-edged sword since the accompanying industry, whilst bringing benefits to ordinary working people, simultaneously extinguished the chances of developing the East Cliff or Wear Bay estate. Such industry inevitably sprang up in association with the railway, for example the SER soon established a coking plant at the 'upper' station as it was still termed. The foul stench from the coking chimneys had to be experienced to be believed, whilst elsewhere the town's gasworks, brickworks, timber yards and fishing interests precluded any hope of smart villas being erected down wind of these industries. Only the West Cliff, high upon the breezy slopes overlooking the English Channel with its 'health-inducing' atmosphere from the prevailing south-westerly winds, fulfilled the dreams and ambitions of Sidney Smirke and Lord Radnor.

At the harbour there were further signs of the industrial wealth being created. Coal was being landed in large quantities with the aid of a new 12hp stationary steam engine which operated two jibs. Two ships, each loaded with 200 tons of coal, could be unloaded within three hours, a half ton coming out on each pan at a time. Folkestone was at a distinct advantage over such ports as Whitstable where 'whippers' - men who manually hoisted out smaller quantities in wicker baskets - were traditionally engaged.

Quite apart from the planned residences for the rich and associated hotels for the well-to-do, accommodation for ordinary folk was not overlooked and fairly soon the town began to spread in all directions. Gradually, Foord became less of a separate hamlet, until 1900 when it had been swallowed up within Folkestone, as were other settlements nearby. In May 1845 the 'Viaduct Cottages', built by Grissell & Peto, were finished, complete with little gardens: 'They have a very pretty effect and a more romantic spot could not possibly have been selected'. It is also revealed that houses opposite the 'upper' station, being built by Mr. Charles Goulder, were also finished, with families ready to move in.

Besides coal and other customary commodities being landed at Folkestone, the more unusual came in from time to time. During May large quantities of rails were landed here before being sent by wagon to Ashford for the completion of the new branch line through the Stour Valley to Canterbury.

Such comings and goings, as well as the regular cross-channel traffic, obviously did much to enliven the town and it is likely that the talk of an evening over a pint of beer was invariably connected with the railway. Towards the end of June there was some considerable excitement about two accidents on the line, mercifully neither causing any deaths, but they were quite spectacular all the same. The first involved a collision between the Night Mail and a train returning from Dover which had just previously conveyed the Duke and Duchess de Nemours on their trip to Ostende. It happened shortly after midnight at Westenhanger when the Dover train was crossing from the down line, back onto the up line, due to engineering work. The Night Mail struck the engine of the up train, tearing up the track and causing both locomotives, as it was quaintly termed, to be 'much injured'. The passengers on board were all considerably shaken, but escaped with only cuts and bruises. However, the engine of the Mail train was able to continue to Dover, whilst the SER subsequently enforced arrangements to prevent such a recurrence.

The second incident was equally as worrying and took place on a Wednesday night when two wagons laden with sleepers were standing on the harbour branch, their brakes pinned down while awaiting an engine to take them down the incline. It had been a wet evening and the rails were greasy, as a result of which the wagons began to move away the moment some of the brakes were released and, rather stupidly, before they could be coupled up to the pilot engine. Gathering speed, they raced down the branch before hitting an empty truck standing on the turntable of the jetty which projected into the inner harbour. The wagon, weighing over two tons, was catapulted over the pier and into the rigging of a schooner where it obviously caused considerable damage.

Efforts to improve facilities were made around that time when workmen began removing old parapet walls in the harbour in preparation for the building of a new and commodious customs house. The *Kent Herald* also commented: 'It is not impossible that the passengers from the railway station [Junction] will be conveyed to the harbour on a tram road, instead of at present by omnibus'. This idea progressed throughout the year, so much so, that by December 1846 the SER. was able to 'state with great confidence' the following:

'Passengers for Folkestone, upon leaving London, will be placed in separate carriages, as in the case of branch lines, and on arriving at Folkestone station, will be conveyed by the tram-road

over a handsome swing bridge which will cross the harbour to the opposite side, into a very large and capacious permanent station to be erected in brickwork.'

Within a matter of a few weeks, workmen were seen driving piles for the foundations of the new swivel bridge which, under Mr. Grissell the contractor, was anticipated would be completed by May 1847. Like so many projects, its construction was not without incident. A foreman walking across the temporary planking to reach a crane called *The Traveller*, missed his footing and fell 30ft into the harbour onto brick rubble. The poor man was reported to be in a 'dangerous state', but thankfully he made an eventual recovery.

Almost anything connected with railways could be considered as potentially dangerous. Frequently it was the company's servants who came to an untimely end, such as John Rayner, the driver of the 4.15pm up train who, for some unrevealed reason, stuck his head out of the cab side to see the road ahead. Unfortunately, the train was just about to enter Shakespeare tunnel, whereupon he was struck by the brickwork of the inclined portal and pitched into the tender. He was eventually carried insensible to the 'Swan Inn' at Dover, but primitive surgical skills could do nothing to save him. Frequently there were accidents involving members of the public, whilst the railways had yet to develop the highly-sophisticated safety rules and regulations which only came about through bitter experience. Many people showed scant regard for their own safety and were in the habit of crossing the tracks or simply wandering alongside as a means of reaching a destination. For example, in March 1846 a workman saved a drunken woman from the wheels of an express after she had staggered into Abbot's Cliff tunnel. Sometimes it seemed that there were mishaps just waiting around the corner. In September 1847 the Down Mail was in the process of bringing down a truckload of oxen for Mr. Worsdell, a Folkestone butcher, when, in passing through Saltwood tunnel, two of them fell out and were subsequently run over by a following light engine. Another occasion involved a pig which broke free from a pen and escaped onto the railway. Pursued by railway staff and the owner who had just paid 17s 0d for it, the unfortunate creature darted across the main line only to be cut in two by the two o'clock mail train.

Apart from everyday accidents such as these, there were often instances of serious theft and petty pilfering. The owner of seven bottles of finest Napoleon brandy was relieved of them when some miscreant forced open a hamper, whilst twenty sovereigns, a handsome sum in those days, were stolen from luggage at the 'upper' station.

Such occurrences, which were almost always published in the most scandalised terms in the local press, were sometimes featured alongside the distinctly peculiar:

'One of the railway porters at Folkestone for a trifling wager, agreed the other day to eat twenty mutton pies each weighing three ounces, in the course of as many minutes. The glutton,

This view of circa 1856 shows the new 'swivel bridge' across the inner harbour which led into the first station — the long building with the overall roof just beyond the clock tower. It was here that the serious runaway accident took place in 1851. Next to the station is the SER's handsome Custom House on the South Quay.

COLLECTION ALAN TAYLOR

having devoured eighteen, was, however, compelled to desist from eating the remainder through being quite sick. (This poor fellow like the rest of the porters, has probably been for some time placed on 'short allowances'.)'

The construction of the swivel bridge, which was intended to carry trains across the harbour whilst allowing ships to enter at high tide, proved more difficult to construct than anticipated. Being, at that time, the largest of its kind anywhere in the world, the hapless engineer had numerous practical problems to overcome. It was already a year behind schedule when, in the spring of 1848, further strengthening work was required to remedy faults in the design, as explained by the *Kent Herald:*

'The new wooden (intended swivel) bridge recently constructed at a large outlay by the South Eastern Railway Co., under their engineer Mr. Bull, is about to assume a novel appearance. Several workmen during the past week have been engaged in erecting stages prior to the alteration of the principle, the ends of the bridge having dropped, so as to fail in acting upon the rollers provided for that purpose. It has therefore been deemed expedient to suspend them by iron rods, so as to keep the sides and centre curved ribs in their respective places. When finished, the bridge may be aptly termed a swivel and suspension bridge.'

April 1848 saw the opening of the Boulogne & Amiens railway, thus making the completion of the Folkestone Harbour branch and its associated improvements all the more pressing and desirable. Nevertheless, before the SER could begin passenger operation over the steeply-graded branch, they were obliged to carry out numerous works and apply to the Board of Trade for their permission. Captain Wynne of the BoT was given the task of conducting experimental runs over the branch to test its suitability, or otherwise, and his final report reads as follows:

'I find all the points to which I referred in my first report have been attended to, viz: the facing points have been removed, a distant signal erected and the brake of the engine made to work more efficiently. I made two or three trips down the incline with a train consisting of a number of carriages and wagons, representing in weight about 24 tons, exclusive of the engine. There was one brake carriage and two wagons having brakes which may be equal together to another brake carriage. I found that descending at a moderate speed the brake of the engine was alone sufficient to bring up the train in a very short distance, but the engine when reversed with so heavy a load was unable to do so. I then tried the power of the carriage brakes, leaving the engine free and found that in a very short distance they likewise efficiently brought up the train. By reducing the train to 16 tons

The SER's fine Harbour House and clock tower. The arms of the SER appear in carved stone above the arch, whilst the tower must have provided a splendid view across the harbour. In the foreground is a newly-constructed horse and carriage dock. To the right is the Pavilion Hotel and, on the cliff behind, the parish church, as well as villas on the eastern Leas.

These two paddle-steamers moored alongside the South Quay were photographed by William Venables in March 1858. The SER favoured round-ended goods wagons, some of which can be seen on the sidings. The buildings in the background comprise the warehouses for the considerable traffic in goods.
COLLECTION ALAN TAYLOR

I found the engine reversed sufficient to stop the train. If, therefore, every fourth carriage in a train is a brake carriage, I consider that such trains may be kept completely under control provided they do not travel at a greater speed than 15mph. With this precaution, in addition to those which the company propose, viz: of stopping all trains before reaching the bridge and ascertaining by the electric telegraph that the bridge is closed before starting a train, I think the branch may be worked with perfect safety and I recommend that the usual certificate allowing it to be opened as a passenger line be granted.'

Accordingly, the Folkestone Harbour branch was duly opened for passenger traffic at the beginning of 1849 as reported in the *Kent Herald* of 18th January:

'The Harbour Station: The new swivel bridge, station and line now used for passenger traffic appears to answer the purpose for which it was intended and the trains run regularly. Much complaint was manifested by the inhabitants, who reside at the top of the town, and who have occasion to travel, at their being brought down to the harbour. This has been remedied: passengers desirous of alighting at the old station can now do so, but as before all passengers for the up trains or for Dover must take tickets at the Harbour station.'

The 'old' station refers to the 'upper' or 'Junction' station as it was later termed. There was also confusion over the timetable bills which were pasted-up advertising the times of trains from Folkestone to Dover. People were arriving at the Harbour station at the specified time, only to find that the bills referred to departures from the Junction and thereby missing their connecting train. There was also discontent at having to change trains at the Junction, as well as 'having to pay extra for the discomfort'. The local paper also advised those travelling to and from the Harbour station by the first or last trains to 'furnish themselves with a lanthorn' as the SER was, in their opinion, 'too parsimonious to use the gas lamps on the harbour'. By all accounts, even the rarely illuminated faces of the grand clock tower were left in darkness for the same reason.

The new station on the south quay, immediately the other side of the 'swivel' bridge, appears to have been opened during 1850. Consisting of two platforms and a canopied roof, both lines led straight towards sets of buffers and the rear wall, beyond which was the beach and sea. Not only was the Harbour station convenient for continental passengers, with just a short walk to the berths on the south pier, but it found favour with locals since at that time most of the town was still centred around that area.

The locomotive history of the Folkestone Harbour branch is interesting if somewhat scant. In his book on SER locomotives, D. L. Bradley revealed that No. 18 *Beult* was used in the early days. Apparently this 0-4-0, built by Bury and dating from 1842, had been used on the Folkestone-London expresses, although of what speed such an early 0-4-0 was capable remains a mystery. Following complaints of rough riding, in the spring of 1844 *Beult* was fitted with sanding gear to aid adhesion, as well as large oak blocks as replacements for buffers, before being despatched to the branch. Other locomotives stated to have been used during the late 1840s were three other Bury 0-4-0s Nos. 107, 108 and 111. It is one of these engines which is believed to have been involved in a serious accident on the Harbour branch during August 1851. At 2.10pm on the afternoon of Tuesday, 12th, the Paris Boat Train began its ascent of the incline on the first part of the journey to London Bridge. There were a number of carriages and luggage vans making up the train which was carrying visitors from the continent as well as homeward-bound Londoners. When it was about halfway up the bank, the coupling between the rear engine and train suddenly parted, whereby the line of carriages began to run backwards and pick up speed. The guards on board immediately screwed down their brakes, but they were quite unable to hinder the heavily-loaded train. Those on board understandably panicked and it was reported that women began screaming. Bystanders watched in horror as the train rushed down the line, expecting it to be 'wholly cast into the sea'. At the Harbour station a quick-witted superintendent directed planks and pieces of timber to be thrown across the tracks in an effort to prevent the train bursting through the terminus. These caused severe jolts to the runaway vehicles and bruised those on board, but its speed was slightly reduced. As the train rumbled into the station, the rear guard leapt for his life at the last moment. The buffer stops were smashed to pieces, as was the rear van which went straight through the station wall, knocking aside a painter who was blissfully working on the exterior quite unaware of events. The second carriage was also badly damaged, but miraculously all the passengers escaped with only varying degrees of contusions when the train was so abruptly halted. Remarkably, in only three hours, calmness had returned and passengers were told to rejoin the train when fresh engines were sent down. Given this introduction to railway travel in England, it isn't surprising to read: 'difficulty was experienced in getting some of the foreigners to take their seats again'.

The Board of Trade viewed the Folkestone accident with deep disquiet, whereby the SER was immediately ordered to ensure that it would never be repeated. Captain Barlow, a superintendent and later General Manager of the SER, instructed that additional brake carriages should be provided. James Cudworth, locomotive superintendent, similarly recommended such action, whereby Richard Mansell, of the Carriage and Wagon department, was 'peremptorily ordered to complete two powerful brakes for the Folkestone Harbour line within one week from this day'. The new brake wagons eventually arrived, but not as quickly as anticipated.

Following the accident, attempts were made to improve the motive power used on the line. During September and October 1851, the SER took delivery of five new 0-4-0s from Robert Stephenson & Co., numbered 152-6. However, they were not particularly well-suited to the branch, suffering from lack of adhesion, especially in wet weather. Indeed, the situation was so unsatisfactory that there were instances when all five engines had to be used in unison to haul a single train up to the Junction. During 1859 they were rebuilt into 0-6-0s, which seems to have improved matters considerably until their eventual replacement in 1877. Locomotive historian Don Bradley considered that another reason for their conversion into 0-6-0s was to spread the weight as they were severely taxing the permanent way of the lightly-laid Harbour branch.

Other precautions taken at this time, which were likely in connection with the recent accident, involved the erection of a footbridge in front of the level crossing outside the Harbour station, as well as a policeman 'in attendance day and night' at the same spot.

Only a few years after the incident involving the Paris Boat Train, yet another runaway made the news on Thursday, 14th December 1854:

> 'On Friday morning last, as the luggage train to Folkestone Harbour was on its way, it ran down with such velocity as to destroy several of the trucks, but fortunately no life was lost, nor did it break through the station into the sea. Since the last accident, a heavy drag machine has been attached to the up and down trains, the brakes having always been worked by two men; and the switchman, who is well acquainted with the spot, has generally in damp weather kept the rails covered with beach stones to check the speed. Now, however, only one man attends the drag machine and in consequence he was unable to work the brake, and the old switchman has been removed.'

Improvements at Folkestone Harbour continued to be forthcoming over the years. In 1854 the foundations were laid for a new Customs House, whilst its completion in 1859 was of sufficient note to make the columns of the *Illustrated London News*. A start was also made on a new pier which projected beyond the old groyne into deeper water to the south-east. However, this pier was subject to all weathers and passengers much preferred using the old south quay whenever possible.

The SER board was well aware of the difficulties in working the Folkestone traffic, hampered by the restrictions caused by the Harbour branch. This probably explains why proposals for a new line in the district received a favourable ear only weeks after the shocking accident of 1851. Unquestionably, the SER looked well beyond the suggestion of a new line, branching away from the vicinity of Westenhanger, to serve Hythe and Sandgate, and gazed instead at the ultimate goal of an extension through to Folkestone harbour. Other schemes followed during 1861 when alternative routes from Cheriton were proposed, one running down through the Pent Valley and beneath Foord viaduct, whereas another was planned to run via Coolinge and Sandgate. The Pent Valley scheme was deemed too costly, whilst the latter line ran into precisely the same objections as the extension of the Sandgate branch, notably from Lord Radnor and other landowners in Folkestone. Throughout 1863 there were protests at the idea of a 'loop line' running alongside the Lower Sandgate Road and across the beach to the harbour. However, the SER evidently thought it could win the day and subsequently went ahead a few years later with the building of the first section to Hythe and Sandgate.

In a probable effort to win back its friends and supporters, the SER favoured the district with another station. Plans entitled 'New Station at Coolinge' were laid before the SER board, whereby platforms and buildings would be erected at the sidings used for the Shorncliffe military traffic which had been laid during 1856. The chosen site was immediately to the west of an overbridge which carried a public road from Broadmead to Coolinge and down into Sandgate. The station building was constructed in brickwork, not timber as thought at one time. Interestingly enough, it survived for an entire century, although used in later years as a goods office. On the opposite platform the SER provided a bay siding and a wooden canopy for the platform. A commodious house, which still stands today and known as 'Wilderness', was provided nearby for the station master. The station was apparently considered not fit enough to receive Prince Arthur of Connaught, who came here on 11th April 1872 on his way to ceremoniously instigate the construction of the Sandgate branch. Following a visit by the chairman and general manager of the SER at the end of February, instructions were issued to provide additional canopies on both platforms, whilst the signal box was to be removed and the platform extended.

Other developments at the start of the 1860s involved the laying of rails along the Stade - the northern side of the harbour where many fishermen's dwellings huddled along the foot of the greensand cliffs. Access to this siding and the subsequent railway workshops at the eastern end was via a small turntable leading directly off the railway viaduct across the inner harbour.

A particularly distressing accident took place shortly before Christmas 1864 when two young women were killed on the railway in the Warren. At a subsequent inquest held at the 'Railway Bell', the coroner recorded a verdict of 'accidental death' after hearing how Mary Wade, aged 17, and her companion Mary Williams, aged 16, had met such a gruesome end. Both were daughters of local coast guards and had been walking along a footpath close to the railway on their way back to Folkestone. For some reason they foolishly decided to walk on the railway, stepping from sleeper to sleeper on the down line. In the meantime the up Continental Mail from Dover had just emerged from Abbot's Cliff tunnel. The fireman first spotted the two girls, who were on the parallel track walking with their backs to the train, but the whistle wasn't sounded as the driver didn't want to cause them to panic. As a strong wind was blowing down the line the girls didn't hear the train until it was very close. Then, when one of them turned and saw the train, instead of remaining on the relative safety of the down line, they immediately ran across in front of it. Although the driver promptly blew his whistle, within a split second they were struck by the locomotive and went beneath its wheels. Passers-by on the seashore paths witnessed the incident unfold with horror, but it fell to the train crew to inspect and report upon the ghastly sight which awaited them.

This is the only known photograph of the first station at Shorncliffe, captured on glass plate in 1871. This view, looking towards Folkestone, shows the porters posed for the photographer, and station master James Keefe standing with his dog next to the roader shed by the up side bay platform. The small signal box can be seen beneath the signal post, set 'clear' for a London train. Curiously, in these early days it was not deemed necessary for the signalman to have a clear view up and down the line. The overbridge carrying Coolinge Lane was demolished in 1881 with the opening of the new Shorncliffe station.
TONBRIDGE HISTORICAL
SOCIETY

Returning briefly to happier matters, the 1860s were years of progress as well as setbacks for both the South Eastern Railway and its rival company, the London, Chatham and Dover Railway, the latter having by 1861 completed its route from Victoria to Dover. Thus the scene was set for some vitriolic showdowns between the competing companies which, alas, benefited neither the unfortunate patrons of their trains, nor their investors and shareholders. During 1865 the 'Continental Agreement' was heralded as something of a victory, whereby the SER and LC&DR agreed to pool receipts on the continental traffic. Although percentages varied from time to time, neither company trusted the other and grew to detest the agreement and began plotting ways to circumvent it through building new stations and projecting other branch lines. Relations between them ranged from grudging co-operation and tolerance to vitriolic hate campaigns in the press.

There also followed blows to the confidence of both companies during the middle of the decade. The SER was considerably shaken when, on Friday 9th June 1865, the Folkestone Tidal Express plunged into the River Beult between Headcorn and Staplehurst. A misunderstanding by a foreman platelayer, due to his ignorance of the 'Tidal' running not at railway time, but at the time of the tide at Folkestone, was the cause of this terrible tragedy. Ten passengers were killed and forty-nine were injured. Among those on board was Charles Dickens and it is said that the great Victorian writer never recovered properly from the appalling ordeal as it wrought such awful damage on his nerves. Friends said he was never the same man again and there may well have been much truth in this for he died in 1870, on the fifth anniversary of the accident.

The SER paid a high price in compensation following the Staplehurst disaster, whilst the LC&DR lost out financially in the following year with the notorious crash in the markets of 1866. At this time the SER was busily engaged in constructing a new main line to Folkestone with the aim of cutting journey times with a more direct route. This new

line, through Chiselhurst, Sevenoaks and Tonbridge was eventually opened to express passenger trains in June 1868. Almost simultaneously, long-overdue improvements were made at Folkestone Junction where the platforms were extended to cater for longer trains. However, the first of many serious slips in the Warren in 1869 put an abrupt end to any feelings of optimism when heavy rain and winter storms further eroded the unstable cliffs.

The problems of the railway through the Warren and those associated with the harbour branch, undoubtedly led to the pursuance of the Sandgate branch, the powers for which had already been obtained during 1864. Railway historians have spoken of this great 'might have been' and rightly so, since the faded records of the SER reveal the true intentions of the day. It was to be a new main line, from Sandling Park, through Seabrook and along the foot of the West Cliff Estate, known as the Lower Sandgate Road. At Folkestone an extensive marine station was to have been built, thus enabling the abandonment of the awkward harbour branch. Confident that it would eventually gain influential support, the SER commenced construction of the branch to Hythe in April 1872, with completion to the temporary terminus two and a half years later.

With the opening of the new double-line to Sandgate, the suffix 'Sandgate' was removed from the nameboards at Shorncliffe, even though this main line station was no less inconvenient to the inhabitants of Sandgate than their new station. In reality, the branch terminated at Seabrook, with a long and sometimes wet walk along the sea wall before the little town was reached. Needless to say, there was considerable clamour for an improvement in the state of affairs, but this was unlikely until Parliament sanctioned the whole new line into Folkestone. However, at one time the SER seriously considered extending the line through to the Broadway in Sandgate purely in the hope of exerting pressure as a second step towards the new Folkestone harbour line. Further incentives in the form of extremely elegant structures in dressed stone, ornamental brick and cast iron for overbridges, footbridges, tunnel entrances and pedestrian walkways were offered. However, the hand-coloured drawings, which were so beautifully produced by the SER's draughtsmen, were never required to be put into anything tangible, but instead remain historical curiosities.

Apart from the Harbour station, which most people preferred, the town was not particularly well-served when it came to convenience of travel. At that time passengers had the choice of alighting at the small Shorncliffe station, which stood in virtual isolation among fields and meadows, continuing to the Junction, which was high up on the hill, or travelling down to the harbour. The emerging west end of the town, where sumptuous villas, houses and hotels were springing up all the time, felt some grievance towards the neglect of their needs. Accordingly, during 1875, ovations were made to the SER concerning a new station at the point where the railway crossed Cheriton Road, half a mile west of the viaduct. The SER, however, was evidently in no mind to lend a favourable ear to Folkestone at this point. A furious row had broken out between those with vested financial interests in the locality of the west end and the SER over its proposals to build the new railway along the foot of the Leas undercliff. Posters proclaiming the 'ruination of Folkestone' were pasted up all over the town as a powerful opposition mustered its forces. In response the SER came up with alternative proposals for driving the new line through a 1¼ mile-long tunnel beneath the Leas, but landowners still refused to have anything to do with it.

While a position of stalemate existed, the SER continued with revisions to the layout at Folkestone Harbour. This was not wasted effort, since trains from either direction, be it the Junction or Sandgate, would make use of the improved facilities. During 1876 the terminus at the harbour was altered so that trains could run onto the new steamer berth at the pier. Much of the land for this had been conveniently provided by the actions of the sea through an accumulation of beach due to the provision of a south-facing groyne. Plans were then put in hand to further improve facilities for passengers.

Yet another blow to the confidence of the SER and its railway through the Warren, came in January 1877 when more winter storms with heavy seas and persistent rain caused the worst landslide to date. The *Folkestone Chronicle* reported that a massive portion of chalk face near Abbot's Cliff had sunk, before sweeping seawards like a huge wave, completely engulfing the railway, filling up the cutting and burying three workmen. One of them, a man named Marsh, knew almost every inch of the line through the Warren and had lived in a little cottage nearby for twenty years. A local reporter mournfully concluded:

'All that is picturesque is gone and the ground, now with the cracks, fissures and rifts which the great shock created, has made it difficult and dangerous for the pedestrian to traverse. The Warren, as Folkestonians and visitors knew it, alas, is now no more.'

The magnitude of the great landslide of January 1877 may be appreciated in this view of workmen in one of the railway cuttings near Abbot's Cliff. With nothing but picks, shovels, wheelbarrows and wagons, it required a huge amount of human effort.
COLLECTION ALAN TAYLOR

The Martello tunnel suffered considerable damage, as witnessed by this photograph, taken by Walter Blackall on 12th January 1877, showing trucks and scaffolding during rebuilding the portal. The opportunity was taken to remove some of the cliff above, thus reducing the likelihood of further problems. In the background is Martello tower No. 3 above Wear Bay. COLLECTION ALAN TAYLOR

Of course, this was not really the case, since within a few years the remarkable regenerative powers of nature simply created a fresh, if somewhat geographically altered, natural paradise. On the other hand, human achievements would not recover so easily and the SER must have questioned the wisdom of building its railway to Dover along this stretch of Kentish coastline. When, on Saturday, 20th January, Sir Edward Watkin travelled down to Folkestone to view the extent of the damage, these thoughts must have been in his mind. About 100 yards of the Martello tunnel had given way, where even the foundations had sunk bodily as the area sagged seawards. Over 900 men were called in, about 50 coming from as far as Portsmouth, to assist in clearing the enormous blockage. The opportunity was taken to cut away much of the chalk cliff above the Dover end of Martello tunnel, which was deposited on the seaward side, thus reducing the weight on the arching. Folkestone Junction station, once so busy, was described as being completely dead, until: 'At night, the scene somewhat changes and when a train of some 18 carriages comes down with its load of navvies the platform is a picture of immense animation'.

Throughout this difficult period the SER arranged for a number of carriages and omnibuses to ply between the towns, whilst help even came from the LC&DR which allowed SER trains to use its main line from Dover to London. In a rare and humble tribute to his counterpart, Sir Edward Watkin publicly stated:

'I must take the opportunity of thanking Mr. Forbes, the chairman of the London, Chatham and Dover Railway, for the facilities he has so kindly and readily rendered in the difficulty under which we have suffered - facilities which have aided us largely in obviating much inconvenience to the general public and delay to Her Majesty's mails.'

After six weeks work, both night and day, the line through the Warren was partially re-opened on Thursday, 8th March, when a pilot engine was sent through with a saloon carriage and two brake vans. Travelling in the saloon was Francis Brady, the SER's chief civil engineer, accompanied by the directors. On leaving Folkestone Junction the train entered Martello tunnel, running on a single line which had been temporarily laid in the centre. As the train approached the site of the greatest landslip near Abbot's Cliff, a long blast was given on the engine's whistle. A stop was made for an inspection of the works, whilst a photographer was able to record the occasion. On this special occasion the locomotive

The first (official) train through the Warren after the 1877 landslide with an array of familiar names associated with the South Eastern. Mr. Newburn (with rolled umbrella) is seen standing alongside the carriage with, behind him, the Hon. James Byng, director, followed by Sir Edward Watkin in the long coat and cap. The figure next to him was Mr. John Shaw, SER secretary (and later general manager), whilst to his left we see Mr. Charles Sheath, personal clerk to Sir Edward (later secretary to SE&CR). The front group features Lord Brabourne, director, wearing a cap and grey coat, and to his immediate right, with a dark beard, Francis Brady, chief engineer, whilst the guard standing in the doorway of van No. 179 was George Privett who was one of the SER's special mail guards. The train comprised Cudworth 'E' class 2–4–0 with stovepipe chimney, a luggage & brake van, a three-compartment 1st class carriage and another luggage van with a low dog compartment.
Photograph and information
CTY. DENIS CULLUM

was driven by Sir Edward Watkin's son Alfred who, following an 'all clear' signal from a linesman, took the train as far as the tunnel before returning to Folkestone.

Not surprisingly, the landslip caused great public excitement, whilst the local paper commented that iron and brass bars were having to be fixed upon carriages to stop passengers poking their heads out of windows in the tunnels to see the work going on. Eventually, both lines were reinstated at the end of May, whereby normal working continued.

During the mid-1870s it was apparent that the 'Bulldog' class tank engines used on the Harbour branch were nearing the end of their useful lives. They were becoming increasingly too small for the traffic being handled, as well as being in need of reboilering. All three were therefore scheduled for replacement with an improved and more powerful design by the SER's locomotive superintendent James Cudworth. He never saw them completed, however, as he retired in October 1876, but they duly arrived at Folkestone in the spring of 1877. All three went into service immediately, two of them being used on the Harbour branch, whilst the third was generally kept busy with working either the Dover goods or the Sandgate branch locals. When operating the Harbour branch, engines always worked smokebox first up the incline, whereas the rules governing the use of brake vans were most rigorously enforced. These ensured that the Tidal Express trains were taken up with two vans, whilst goods trains required one van for every three loaded wagons. It was generally considered that these instructions were sufficient; indeed, it appears the branch had been worked safely on this principle for almost a quarter of a century. However, on the morning of 27th February 1878, an up goods train consisting of wagon loads of recently landed fish, suddenly parted just as it was nearing the Junction station. Much to the probable

horror of the train's guard, the brakes on the van proved ineffective on this occasion, whereby it was propelled backwards down the branch until, at about ten miles an hour, it collided with tank engine No.152. The brakesman was slightly injured in the shock on impact, but was reasonably fortunate considering that his van and the fish trucks were almost completely wrecked.

The invention of the vacuum brake, whereby trains would be brought to a halt should they part, was undoubtedly a great step forward in railway development and safety. The Tidal Express had been effectively protected in this manner since June 1875, but the SER had still to fit such brakes to the Harbour branch locomotives. In spite of criticism from the Board of Trade, engines with vacuum brakes were not introduced on the branch until 1892 and it is perhaps astounding that resistance to such an obvious requirement lasted for so long.

Accidents on the railways around Folkestone happened from time to time and made the news accordingly. There were instances of broken limbs at the harbour, drownings and sometimes more horrifying accidents, such as shunters being crushed between wagons in a moment's carelessness. In October 1878 a fireman was engaged in changing a headlamp on a train at Shorncliffe station when he slipped, fell beneath the wheels and lost both his legs. The SER eventually awarded him twenty pounds compensation, but the poor fellow's future must have seemed frighteningly bleak.

With the dawn of 1880 the new decade brought promises of greater improvements to the railways of Folkestone. For some time the board of directors had looked towards rectifying the position at Shorncliffe station where the cramped and insufficient facilities were ill-suited to the amount of traffic now being generated by the military camp. Although Sandgate station was well-used by soldiers

One of the Cudworth-designed 0–6–0T locomotives of 1877 crossing the swing bridge with a train of empty wagons c.1881-2. The iron restraining braces on the bridge were a necessary addition to the original design and effectively prevented the ends of the span from sagging. Trains from Folkestone Harbour were signalled for departure from both platforms. The sidings on the right led towards the Stade where a wagon turntable enabled a 90° turn towards the workshops seen at the far right of the picture. The after saloon of Napoleon III is nearest the camera, whilst beyond we see two sailing coasters, Julia and Hannah, followed by a small cargo paddle steamer Alexandra, built by Samuda Bros. in 1864, and finally the largest vessel, Duchess of Edinburgh, next to the gridiron. Along the Stade can be seen the fish market where daily catches were sold, as well as the premises of rope and sail makers, net makers and, of course, purveyors of 'Fine Ales and Porter'. L&GRP

returning to barracks, it was felt that a new station was needed. It must be admitted that the reasons for reconstructing Shorncliffe on a new site and on such a large and lavish scale were not entirely honest, the SER having ulterior motives carefully concealed up its corporate sleeve. Even so, the Board of Trade was not concerned with the skullduggery of railway politics when asked to inspect the new station in December, nor were the people of Folkestone who heartily welcomed this extensive addition.

Before creating the new station, the SER was obliged to apply for the diversion of various footpaths and roadways, the most obvious change being the demolition of Coolinge overbridge. The old down platform wasn't removed until many years later which explains the generous space between the down main line and what later became the Elham Valley, or down local line. On the opposite side, part of the original up platform was incorporated into a new goods depot, whilst the former station building of 1863 became a goods office. On the Folkestone side of the demolished overbridge, new platforms were laid down either side of four lines of railway where loop roads were created, thus allowing fast, through running. A complete revision of the trackwork and signalling required the provision of two cabins, No.1 (West) and No.2 (East), containing 21 and 11 working levers respectively.

Reading between the lines, Major Marindin, who inspected the station on behalf of the BoT, appeared quite taken aback by its sheer size and grandiose opulence, but was nevertheless full of praise for its 'very good accommodation'. He did, however, express concern that the awning columns were a little too near the platform edging and asked for clocks to be placed in the signalboxes, clocks outside the station, and nameboards to be put up as soon as possible. It seems evident that the SER was in a hurry to open the station since painters were seen busily working everywhere. This gracious station, which finally opened as 'Shorncliffe Camp' on 1st February 1881, was a delight to behold, comprising a connecting subway, fully-glazed canopies over the platforms and forecourts, refreshment rooms, booking offices, parcels offices, separate waiting rooms, and conveniences on both sides. Elegant cast-iron columns with decorative supports featuring leaves and fruit created a wonderful effect, whilst the warm orange-red tone of the brickwork contrasted beautifully with the pale cream stonework and painted, decorative woodwork. Windows with half-rounded tops made the rooms light and airy, whilst some were even embellished with stained glass, proudly depicting the SER coat of arms.

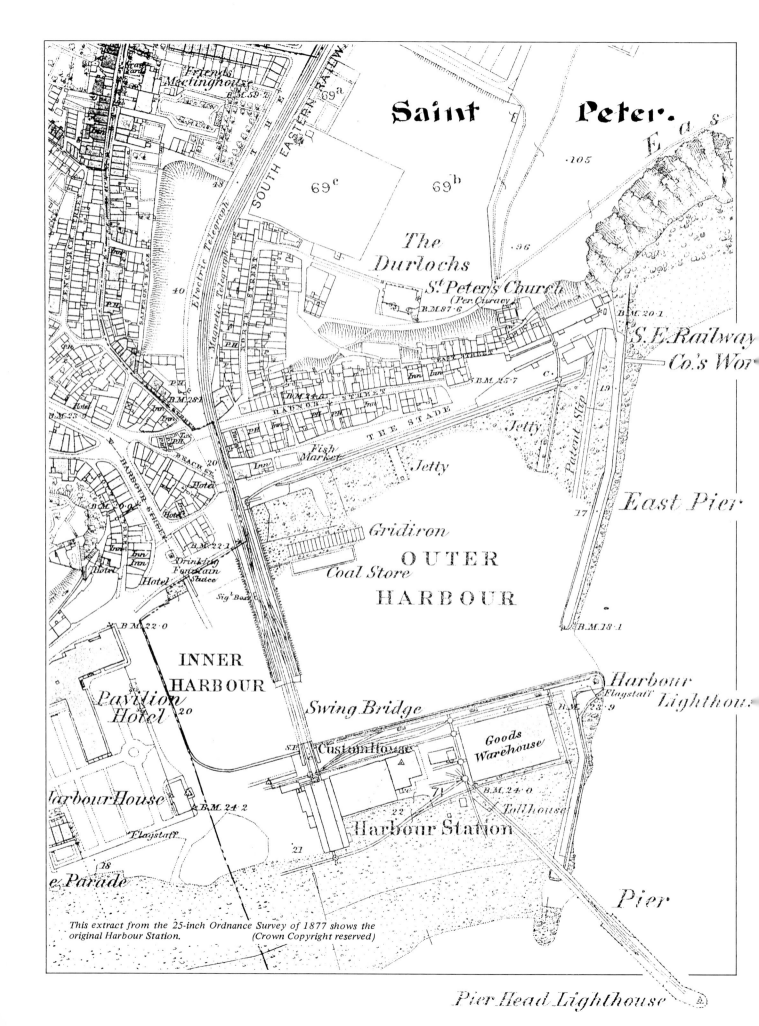

Saint Peter.

The Durlochs

69^c

69^b

·105

·96

SOUTH EASTERN RAILWAY

Friends Meetinghouse

B.M.59·2

48

Electric Telegraph

Magnetic Telegraph

40

St Peter's Church
(Per. Curacy)

B.M.87·6

·E. & S.

B.M.20·1

S.E.Railway Co.'s Wor

19

B.M.25·7

C.

Jetty

Patent Slip

THE STADE

Jetty

17

East Pier

Fish Market

B.M.28·1

B.M.23·

Hotel

P.H.

P.H.

P.H.

P.H.

Drinking Fountain Sluice

B.M.22·1

Gridiron

Coal Store

OUTER

HARBOUR

B.M.18·1

B.M.22·0

Sig.l Box

INNER

HARBOUR

Pavilion Hotel

20

Swing Bridge

Harbour Lighthouse

Flagstaff

B.M.23·9

Goods Warehouse

Custom House

Harbour House

B.M.24·2

Flagstaff

71

B.M.24·0

Tollhouse

22

Harbour Station

28

e Parade

21

Pier

This extract from the 25-inch Ordnance Survey of 1877 shows the
original Harbour Station.   (Crown Copyright reserved)

Pier Head Lighthouse

A marvellous view of the Inner Harbour at Folkestone, taken in the mid-1880s. The name on the furthest sailing ship is Enterprise, *whilst the identity of the elegant paddle-steamer is unknown. In the background, the steep incline towards Folkestone Junction is appreciated where the line curves to the right near Tolputt's chimney. Nearby is the protecting bracket signal for the railway pier, controlled by the small, typically SER, signal box at the end of the adjacent sidings. This view shows how much the town had grown around the Pent stream which flows into the harbour behind the steamer.*
COLLECTION ALAN TAYLOR

Accompanying the grandeur now associated with Shorncliffe, a new road into Folkestone was laid down. This wide, tree-lined avenue was deemed to be a far more appropriate entrance into the town where the titled and wealthy visitors to Folkestone might ride in their glossy black carriages to plush hotels without being offended by gazing upon the more humble, malodorous and industrious areas gathered around the harbour. The *Folkestone Chronicle* rather gave the game away when it noted:

'The opening of the new station at Shorncliffe is an event that deserves a passing notice. It shows the great anxiety of the South Eastern to minister to the convenience of the visitors to Folkestone and the inhabitants of the West End. It has been stated that the Company manifest their concern chiefly in the continental traffic. The building of this station, and the magnificent road to it, is a refutation to this statement.'

The construction of Shorncliffe station, coupled with the directors' support for the latest proposals for a tramway along Shorncliffe Road to connect with the town and harbour, led the SER's opponents to deduce that the company's cover had been blown. Critics viewed it as nothing more than an attempt to circumnavigate the Continental Agreement of 1865. The LC&DR soon retaliated, not only by commencing legal proceedings with a lawsuit, which the SER eventually lost, but also in resurrecting its Alkham Valley Railway scheme. It must be said that the SER had good reason to be worried by the threat of this proposed branch line from Kearsney since the LC&DR was already building a line from Maidstone to Ashford - right into the very heart of the SER's empire. Then, in March, it was reported that surveyors

'employed by the Chatham company' were at Ruckinge, a tiny hamlet 5 miles south of Ashford on the edge of Romney Marsh 'for extending the Maidstone and Ashford railway to possibly Dungeness harbour'. Alarmed by the prospect of the LC&DR attempting to build a new harbour on the South Coast, the SER apparently responded for the same newspaper carried a small piece which revealed:

'An engineer employed by the SER has been engaged within the past day or two stumping out the land for the extension of the Hythe and Sandgate branch to Folkestone Harbour. Tenders for the contracts will shortly be issued and the work commenced at once.'

Along with the new Shorncliffe station, the SER had also taken the precaution of reviving the powers of the erstwhile Elham Valley Light Railway Company which had originally proposed a line from Hythe to Canterbury. These were revised to allow a connection into the main line at Cheriton which obviously pleased Folkestone since the Town Clerk presented a draft petition in favour of the Elham Valley Bill. The Royal Assent was granted in the autumn of 1881; however, throughout the following two years the scheme remained moribund until the LC&DR clarified its intentions.

Partly in conjunction with the new Shorncliffe station, the SER considered building a branch line directly into the barracks, notably for handling supplies and transporting horses. They considered such a development would be a distinct advantage. Even so, the War Office was disinclined to lend financial support whereby the idea eventually fell by the wayside.

Another landslip in the Warren occurred during March 1881 when tons of chalk came sliding down once more at Abbot's Cliff. The four o'clock mail train had only recently passed through, whereas watchmen had to halt the Brussels express which left Dover at 5.30pm. Within two days, though, the line had been sufficiently cleared for normal traffic.

There were varying proposals for railways of all kinds coming forward at this time, some quite modest, whilst others were grand in the extreme. A new water-balance lift in the Pyrenees had captured the imagination of recent visitors and suggestions were made for a similar cliff railway running down the Leas cliff. On a far more momentous scale, Sir Edward Watkin came down to inspect Colonel Beaumont's machine for digging the Channel Tunnel. During July, Watkin, as well as numerous dignitaries associated with the North of France Railway, rode on trolleys along the half-mile tunnel which was stated to run 90ft beneath Abbot's Cliff and parallel with the railway above. Captain English explained to the party, who were dressed in canvas and serge coats, the workings of their patented contraption which he boasted could cut through the chalk at half an inch per minute. Afterwards, they went on to inspect the 150ft shaft sunk at Shakespeare Cliff where the tunnel would commence running beneath the English Channel. Luncheon at the Lord Warden Hotel in Dover provided a pleasant conclusion to the morning's somewhat dank and gloomy experience at which Sir Edward optimistly announced to much cheering and applause that he was: 'sanguine and obstinate enough to believe that he should live to see the tunnel completed and many of those present riding in it.'

Developments were also under way at the harbour where, on Wednesday, 15th October 1881, HRH Edward, Prince of Wales, laid the ceremonial stone at the commencement of the new railway pier. The event coincided with the opening of Prince's Parade, his Royal Highness having arrived at Hythe station at midday, to be greeted by crowds lining the route along the seafront where the extensive but ill-fated Seabrook Estate was planned. After lunch at the Pavilion Hotel, Prince Edward returned to London via the new Shorncliffe station which had been gaily decorated for the occasion.

Work on the enlarged new pier at Folkestone, which included extended platforms for trains to run further seawards, reached completion in 1883. For a time, the facilities here were thought superior to those available at Dover. Passenger traffic was then transferred to the new pier, with the old South Pier, in front of the grand customs house, being used mainly for cargo steamers. Proposals for an eastern breakwater, projecting from Copt Point at the East Cliff, were never taken up in spite of numerous surveys and plans over the decades.

Surprisingly, the forming of the 'Folkestone, Sandgate and Hythe Tramway Co. Ltd' during the autumn of 1883 sparked off yet another battle in the long-running feud between the SER and LC&DR. The reason for this was that the street tramways of the FS&HT Company, some of which were intended to run along Shorncliffe Road, would be in direct physical conflict with the LC&DR's scheme for an Alkham Valley Line, scheduled to terminate in the heart of the West End - and closer than Shorncliffe! In an effort to bolster its support for the FS&HT Co., the SER promptly picked up its dormant Elham Valley powers and announced the immediate construction of a double-track railway from Folkestone to Canterbury, thus, in its opinion, doing away with any need for an Alkham Valley Line. Well into the spring of 1884 arguments positively raged, with posters being pasted-up all over Folkestone, the overwhelming majority against the LC&DR and in favour of the SER. It was rather ironic that the SER, which had only recently been the villain of the piece in attempting to extend the Sandgate branch to the harbour, should suddenly find so many friends and supporters in high places. Councillor Wedderburn declared himself in favour of railways, but wholly against the LC&DR's Alkham Valley terminus 'You may have the Great Northern, the Great Western and the Great Eastern as far as I'm concerned - but don't spoil the West End of the town'. However, the LC&DR considered Folkestone would be far better served with a new line from Kearsney where a triangular junction would give easy access to both Dover and Canterbury, as well as providing another direct route to London. The 'Chatham's' considered that the SER's line through the Warren was constantly under threat from nature, whilst their Alkham Valley Line would put an end to such disruptions and chaos once and for all. Criticism was also aimed at their counterparts on the SER for having connived so disgracefully to avoid the Continental Agreement in building the new Shorncliffe station. Myles Fenton, general manager of the SER, flatly denied the insinuation that it had deliberately been built to draw traffic away from Folkestone, claiming that its primary purpose was to serve the military camp. However, he wasn't able to explain why soldiers should have been treated to such opulence or why they might need, for that matter, so much in the way of ladies' accommodation! In attacking the LC&DR's scheme, Fenton somewhat hypocritically remarked: 'A beautiful valley will be cut up, unsightly embankments raised, the neighbourhood of Foord interfered with, as well as the ruination of the West End'. He further contended that the SER had been 'the best friend to Folkestone' and cited all the rewards their railway had secured. Most people seemed to agree with him, one correspondent writing to say it shouldn't be forgotten how the SER had benefited the 'labouring classes' at the harbour. Accordingly, Folkestone threw its weight behind the South Eastern but, in doing so, left the directors with little alternative other than to honour their part of the agreement by pressing ahead with the very costly construction of a main line to Canterbury via the Elham Valley.

With the SER so anxious to please Folkestone, it might come as no surprise that an enquirer who requested a station that was more central to the town should have received no less than a personal assurance from Watkin that it would be investigated. Anything to baulk the SER's counter attack

An interesting, if hazy, glimpse of a down train entering the western end of Cheriton Arch station. Taken about 1886, the locomotive appears to have been one of Cudworth's '118' class 2–4–0s which provided the mainstay of SER motive power at this period. The unusual design of the signal box was a departure from the familiar pattern adopted by the SER and is somethng of a surprise.

against the threat from the LC&DR's proposal would apparently be favourably looked upon. Within a matter of weeks a site was chosen just to the west, or Shorncliffe side, of Cheriton Road where a narrow brick arch carried the railway. Viewed as an additional nail in the coffin of the Alkham Valley Line, construction of 'Cheriton Road', as it was originally called, progressed rapidly throughout the summer. This new stopping place, which Major Marindin came down to inspect on 8th August 1884, merely comprised platforms on either side of the tracks with station offices and a signalbox on the down side at the London end. The BoT report stated:

'CHERITON ROAD: There are no connections at this station but signals in both directions★ and block telegraph instruments have been provided and there is sufficient platform and other accommodation.

The name boards have not yet been put up as there has been some doubt as to the name to be adopted.

These have now been ordered.'

★A 7-lever frame comprising 2 distants, 2 home, 2 starting signals and 1 spare

Accordingly, for want of a better name, the new station opened as 'Cheriton Arch' ten days later, on 18th August, with three up trains calling at: 9.0am, 11.55am and 5.29pm, whilst in the down (Dover) direction departures were advertised at 8.44am, 9.58am, 12.55pm, 6.37pm and 10.7pm. On Sundays only two trains called, viz: 7.45am (up) and 10.51am (down).

A further ten days hence, on 28th August, Sir George Russell, performed the ceremonial honours in a field at Newington at the commencement of the Elham Valley Line. In fact, work had already begun on this expensive line to Canterbury, navvies having previously made a start on the deep cutting through Etchinghill.

Whilst matters were progressing on the new Canterbury branch, the prospects for the Channel Tunnel were distinctly less healthy. All work had ceased and there seemed no chance of Colonel Beaumont's celebrated chalk cutting machine moving another inch towards France as revealed in the press:

'Most people were pleased to learn that Sir Edward Watkin's Utopean scheme of the Channel Tunnel has come to an end. There was an overwhelming majority against the Bill in the House of Lords. Our military, scientific and commercial men are against it. Those who support it consist of a few experimentalists and crotcheteers. In any case, the Government would be obliged to maintain an armed guard at the tunnel mouth, in constant fear of it.'

Railways seemed to fill the news in 1884 and before the year was out there was talk of yet three other schemes devised and promoted by Watkin, yet none was taken very seriously. One envisaged a line from Seabrook to New Romney, another, an extension from Sandgate via the military camp to Shorncliffe station, whilst a third sought to do away with the awkward and steeply-inclined Harbour branch by reviving the idea of a new line from Cheriton, descending to pass through the Foord viaduct and on towards the seashore.

In September 1885 a most novel railway opened in Folkestone, the first of four such cliff railways which operated on the ingenious water-balance principle. The installation, which survives to this day and remarkably still runs on the same method, fascinated strollers on the Leas and provided them with an easy ascent from the foreshore. Indeed, it proved so popular that a second lift was built adjacent, opening just five years later.

Another curious line, and one far less well-known, was the railway which ran for almost a mile from the goods yard at Shorncliffe to the Pleasure Gardens Theatre. This building, which was demolished in the 1960s, was designed on a grand scale with twin turrets and a large semi-circular roof. Its original purpose was to house the National Art Treasures Exhibition, opened on 22nd May 1886 by the Lord Mayor of London. Building materials for its construction were conveyed to the site by rail, using track destined eventually for the Elham Valley. The line, running on virtually level ground along Shorncliffe Road, crossed Earl's Avenue, before terminating in the grounds at the rear of Ingle's meadow. To enable passengers to be conveyed from Shorncliffe to the temporary platform, necessitated authorization from the BoT. Major Hutchinson insisted that only one engine at a time should work the branch, at no greater speed than 6mph, with no propelling of passenger trains. Bars across roads at Shorncliffe and Earls Avenue were necessary, as was a crossing keeper at the latter road. A single line staff token was also required, whilst Mr. Cheeseman, station master at Shorncliffe, was to have personal charge over the line and its train. The *Hythe & Sandgate Advertiser* commented on the opening day:

'The members of the London press came down by the mail at 12.30 on Wednesday in carriages specially provided for them through the courtesy of Mr. Myles Fenton, the general manager of the SER. At Shorncliffe these carriages were slipped and from thence the visitors travelled by special train, in charge of Mr. John Cheeseman, along the branch line over the arable land to the exhibition. Here they were received by His Worship the Mayor.....'

The LC&DR promptly threatened legal action if the receipts from the traffic over the spur weren't pooled. However, the success of the exhibition failed anticipations with the result that the SER's revenue amounted to less than

£11,000. Mr. Cheeseman was duly awarded £25 'in recognition of his services', but by the following spring the branch line was dismantled and transported for use along the Elham Valley Line.

The daily business around the harbour was once again disrupted during July when the brakes on a heavily-laden goods train failed as it approached East Cliff crossing. The crew frantically tried to halt the runaway, which reached an estimated 40mph, before colliding with a 'special fruit train' in the harbour station. Although the fireman jumped clear, whilst the driver remained at the controls, both men were extremely lucky and escaped serious injury.

In October 1886 a rather curious affair took place, related by Don Bradley in his book on South Eastern locomotives. Apparently a passenger became suspicious of the engine crew of 0-6-0T No.152 and informed H. M. Customs. Upon inspection, eleven bottles of brandy were found concealed within the coal bunker, whereby the driver and fireman were promptly arrested and charged with smuggling. They were eventually fined as well as being dismissed from the company's service, whilst events then proceeded to take on a farcical turn when the authorities deemed No.152 equally culpable in the eyes of the law. As a result it spent a month on the quayside, its footplate boarded up and its wheels and motion firmly secured with chains. Don went on to relate: 'For a time it seemed highly probable that the South Eastern Railway would be fined for the engine's part in the affair, but saner councils prevailed and No.152 re-entered service with its character unblemished'!

The summer of 1887 witnessed the opening of the first section of the Elham Valley Line as far as Barham. Three new stations were brought into use on Monday, 4th July, at Lyminge, Elham and Barham. However, until the line opened throughout to Canterbury, a shuttle service operated between Shorncliffe Camp and Barham with six trains each way on weekdays and three on Sundays. These trains used an independent single line between Shorncliffe Camp and Cheriton where the route diverged and headed towards Etchinghill and the Elham Valley.

Other developments around this time were concerned with generally improving the standard of service to Folkestone. In September 1886 the name 'Cheriton Arch' had been dropped in favour of 'Radnor Park' which seemed even less helpful to visitors in describing its position or relationship to the town. A more frequent train service to benefit the area was requested following the opening, on New Year's Day 1888, of Sandling Junction station, where the Sandgate branch diverged from the main line. At one time the SER even considered building a station at Cheriton Junction, to coincide with the opening of the Elham Valley route to Canterbury, but the idea never progressed. Similarly, suggestions for a station on the new branch at Newington failed to be taken up. However, a halt had been opened in the Warren during the summer of 1886, presumably to cater for the occasional band of excursionists. When, in 1888, Major General Hutchinson of the Board of Trade was idly thumbing

The provision of covered footways from the road to the cramped Radnor Park station are shown under construction in this glass plate photograph taken in May 1890. TONBRIDGE HISTORICAL SOCIETY

through his copy of Bradshaw's, he became curious and subsequently penned an internal memo: 'In the Bradshaw, page 97, I see a new station between Folkestone and Dover called 'Folkestone Warren' - has this ever been inspected? No notice of it has ever been received, - is it a station at the junction of the Harbour Branch?' - to which he received the reply: 'No, it is on the undercliff between Folkestone and Dover – I think the company should be asked for an explanation!' An abrupt letter was promptly despatched to the general manager of the SER. Myles Fenton offered a rather feeble excuse, explaining that as the halt had been used by only a few excursion parties, they thought it unnecessary to inform the Board, adding that in any case the trains hadn't stopped there since 29th September. Throughout the spring of 1889 workmen were seen at the Warren Halt erecting a footbridge, not only for the convenience of its patrons, but to enable the seashore to be reached from the cliff paths on the other side of the line. The new halt was subsequently inspected by the BoT in August 1889, but curiously was never officially sanctioned for public use until almost twenty years later in 1908.

The opening of the Elham Valley Line to Canterbury, on 1st July 1889, was certainly a day for celebration since Folkestone was now served by railways from three directions. At Cheriton a new junction was created. This led from the 'up' line onto the branch, whilst the former single line became an independent 'down' road to Shorncliffe for Elham Valley trains.

Interestingly enough, in the previous year, Sir Edward Watkin had approached the LC&DR to seek their directors' opinion on the possibilities of eventually connecting the Elham Valley into their London-Dover line. Unfortunately, the idea was rejected, which is a pity since both routes would undoubtedly have benefited from the creation of a direct Folkestone to London (Victoria) link. Instead, the line swung into the Ashford-Canterbury branch at Harbledown Junction whereby a double-track railway, well-engineered to main line standards, inevitably became an under-used backwater throughout its entire sixty-years' existence.

After a protracted battle of at least a decade, the Folkestone, Sandgate and Hythe Tramway Company managed to open the first section of its horse-drawn system in May 1891. This commenced running from the Seabrook (later 'Imperial') Hotel to the western end of Sandgate. Further extensions to Red Lion Square in Hythe and through Sandgate to the foot of the hill leading up to Folkestone were opened in the following year. Intended to be the first stage of an expansive electric tramway system serving the whole of Folkestone, it similarly met with concerted opposition from landowners.

During 1892 Ashford Railway Works completed three further members of James Stirling's 'R' class 0-6-0 tank engines. These were destined to replace the earlier 'Folkestone' tanks of 1877 which were at the end of their days. By July, 'R's nos. 152, 153 and 154 arrived at Folkestone where they immediately took over from the older locomotives which bore the same numbers. The new

Low tides at Folkestone restricted larger steamers docking at the South Quay. Accordingly in 1863, a new pier was constructed, but passengers disapproved of the often wet and windy walk to the ships. In March 1876 the SER opened the 'New Channel Station' which included offices and canopied platforms which can be seen on the foreshore, just by the stone groyne under construction. An extension of the railway lines onto the pier necessitated slewing the original harbour terminus buildings in a sharp curve as depicted here. In 1881, further expansion and development of the new pier then gave Folkestone superior facilities to those on offer at Dover. This view, taken about 1895, admirably shows how the harbour had continued to grow. Notice also the new carriage sidings on the beach which were laid in 1893.

COLLECTION ALAN TAYLOR

The outer harbour from the South Quay. Apart from the paddle-steamer moored near the grid-iron, the fishing boats enliven this scene taken about 1897. COLLECTION ALAN TAYLOR

One of Stirling's powerful new 'R' class locomotives blowing off steam while waiting with a train as Duchess of York *reverses away from the extended pier in the summer of 1897.* COLLECTION ALAN TAYLOR

A rare glimpse of East Cliff Crossing, halfway up the harbour incline, with an 'R' class bringing a rake of empty carriages down the branch.

The ship repair yards in the outer harbour with a variety of paddle-steamers in evidence. The small, elegant single-funnelled vessel in the centre was either the delightful Myleta *or* Edward William*, both of which were used for pleasure trips along the coast, as well as the SER's Port Victoria–Sheerness services across the River Medway. Folkestone was a thriving semi-industrial town at this time.*

engines, being heavier and far more powerful, soon proved themselves to be very successful in moving the boat trains from the Harbour station up to the Junction. Nos. 152-4 remained at Folkestone for a further six years until they were re-allocated to other depots. Incidentally, Don Bradley commented that No. 153 retained for a while its gold anchor which was painted on the smokebox door and doubtless applied by a keen railwayman. From 1898, though, their place was taken by Nos. 69, 70 and 107.

Another quite unique railway opened in Folkestone in 1893. This was the Sandgate Hill Lift which was less like a traditional cliff lift since it operated on comparatively easy gradients ranging from 1 in 4¾ to 1 in 7. Running from the westernmost end of the Leas, across Radnor Crescent and almost to the bottom of Sandgate Hill, it provided a most useful link to the SER's horse tram to Hythe. This unusual railway, with its beautifully constructed buildings and delightfully ornate cars, soon proved very popular with the fashionable visitors to Folkestone; for example, during August Bank Holiday Monday of that year over 3,000 people travelled upon it.

A major item of engineering was renewed on the Harbour branch during 1892-3 when the swing bridge was replaced, the original 'suspension and swivel' span being by then over forty years old. The new one, weighing around 150 tons, was constructed in steel as well as wood in order to carry the heavier trains now running over the branch. Also, around this

time, the SER laid out extensive carriage sidings to the west of the Harbour station on the shingle foreshore.

1894 was undoubtedly the end of an era since it brought the retirement of Sir Edward Watkin, then aged 74. This 'railway giant' of the Victorian age had worldwide connections with railways, but perhaps he is most associated with the SER due to his long chairmanship. Watkin was also very much involved with the town itself, and represented Hythe in Parliament for a time. For good or bad, his relatively modest dream of extending the Sandgate branch and later attempts to build other routes to Folkestone Harbour remained unfulfilled. Perhaps the district benefited or suffered as a result - who can say for certain? However, his greatest and most cherished ambition - a railway tunnel beneath the English Channel - finally arrived, albeit nearly a century after his death. The people of Folkestone eventually took him to their hearts, whilst he was at least honoured with having a road named after him, as were Sir George Russell and Sir Cosmo Bonsor, fellow directors of the old South Eastern.

Improvements at Radnor Park station were deemed appropriate during 1895. Although, five years earlier, work had been undertaken to roof over the walkways leading up to the platforms from Cheriton Road, the station was not particularly inviting to passengers. It was decided that the name needed changing, 'Radnor Park' having been chosen at the same time as a large area of adjacent land had been gifted

This late Victorian panorama shows some of the activity involving ships, carts and cargo which went on at this time. The vessel nearest the camera is marked 'Seamen's Mission', whilst huge lengths of timber can be seen stacked behind it.
COLLECTION ALAN TAYLOR

to the town by His Lordship for landscaping and recreation purposes. Also, fashionable houses had sprung up all around the locality, whilst the West End of the town had become *the* place to be during the fashionable summer season. Renamed 'Folkestone Central' on 1st June 1895, simultaneous improvements were carried out. These involved the widening of platforms, the provision of a new bay on the up side so that portions could be attached to London services, as well as a general spruce-up, eventually amounting to more than £10,000. Gradually, Folkestone Central usurped the role of Shorncliffe as the premier station and, in later years, enjoyed the benefits of seeing all the best express trains stopping there.

Other stations serving the towns similarly witnessed gradual improvements over the years. Goods traffic was the most important business at Folkestone Junction so extensive facilities were provided where the old coking ovens had been. The production of coke for railway engines had ceased in the 1880s when coal-burning was perfected, a decision which cannot have proved popular with despairing housewives whose Monday wash was periodically ruined by the Harbour branch engines! A considerable amount of goods traffic was also managed at Shorncliffe, notably in dealing with the military camp, whilst in 1898 a siding for the coal traffic was laid into the adjacent Folkestone Electric Company Works.

Towards the end of the century, work began on a major reconstruction of Folkestone Harbour, notably the widening and extension of the pier which was rebuilt for the most part in granite blocks brought in by ships. Track re-modelling also took place, as well as the re-designing of the station facilities there. Sadly, the Harbour House with its fine clock tower, erected half a century before, was deemed dispensable and was demolished as the land was needed for the approach to the improved station.

As the long reign of Queen Victoria began to draw to an end, Folkestone's railways became part of the SE&CR system, following the eventual working union between the once-feuding companies. Ahead stood the twentieth century, and an age of even greater upheaval, during which time the railway would continue to play an important and significant role.

Folkestone has traditionally been famous for its catches of fresh fish from the English Channel. Here, another load was being taken ashore to be sold at the slabs on the Stade.

COLLECTION ALAN TAYLOR

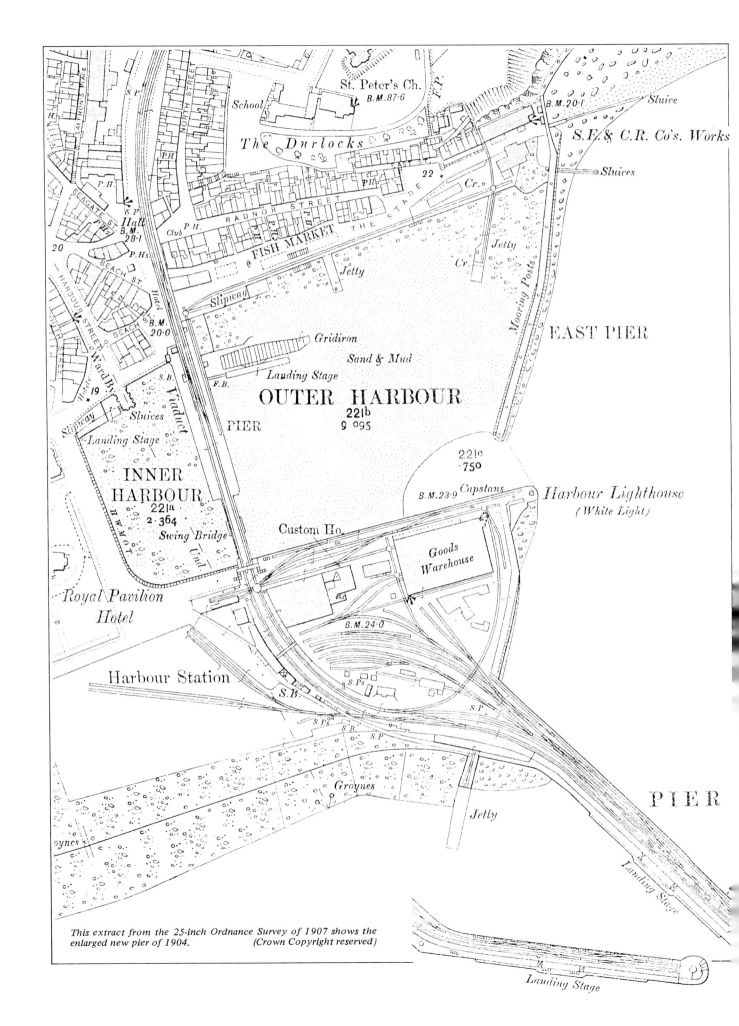

This extract from the 25-inch Ordnance Survey of 1907 shows the
enlarged new pier of 1904.   (Crown Copyright reserved)

CHAPTER FOUR
THE GLORIOUS CENTURY

BARELY had the twentieth century begun when, in 1901, the demise of Queen Victoria, as well as Sir Edward Watkin, seemed to bring to a conclusion a colourful chapter of English life. Many other old and familiar faces had similarly passed away, but were soon replaced by new figures who would likewise become household names.

Changes were taking place on the railway, especially at the harbour where the new pier and station were rapidly taking shape. Completion in 1904 almost coincided with the arrival of the powerful turbine steamers, the first of these, *The Queen*, being brought into service the previous year when introduced on the Folkestone-Boulogne service. Gradually, the fleet of ageing but extremely elegant paddle steamers was withdrawn, the last reputed to have gone in 1911.

Edwardian Folkestone - simply *the* place to be seen - reached its pinnacle of prosperity as trainloads of society people eagerly poured into the town during the high summer season. Graceful express locomotives, notably Stirling's beautiful 'A', 'B' and 'F' 4-4-0 classes steamed into the Central station and formed the main attraction for almost every Edwardian boy. In their livery of lined-out deep Brunswick green paintwork, they simply gleamed, whilst their polished brasswork positively glinted in the bright sunshine as safety valves deafeningly lifted to release pent-up steam. A veritable army of porters scurried everywhere, unloading the almost countless items of luggage - hat boxes, trunks, Gladstone bags and portmanteaux - all of which had to be conveyed to the plush hotels which dominated the exclusive Leas. Horse-drawn traps and the new motor landaulets created a traffic jam as they manoeuvred themselves out of the cramped approach road and along Castle Hill Avenue towards the West Cliff estates and tree-lined squares patronised by the upper and middle classes.

The scene at Shorncliffe was often just as busy, but most notably with the heavy traffic being dealt with at the camp. Here, a train in the platform would load-up with its khaki-clad human cargo who would pour forth from the large refreshment rooms leaving behind blushing tea-girls. Often it might have to wait upon the passing of an express which would come thundering through, rattling teacups and glasses, as it confidently gathered pace on the run to London. In the goods yard an engine would invariably be pottering about, clattering the collection of wagons into order, whilst a couple of goods porters might do their best to coax a stubborn horse into its railway horsebox. Every now and then the local train would arrive, calling at Sandling Junction, Westenhanger and Smeeth on its way to Ashford. Other trains, carrying seasonal visitors and keen excursionists, were destined for the picturesque villages of Lyminge, Elham, Barham, Bishopsbourne, and Bridge before reaching the ancient city of Canterbury.

Across the other end of town, beyond the Foord viaduct which stood majestic above the many smoking chimney pots of the huddled houses and cramped backyards below, the scene at Folkestone Junction was always one of incessant activity. Apart from the Dover expresses which wound their way beneath the towering cliffs of the Warren, the Harbour branch remained busy with the passenger and goods trains which had to be heaved up the tortuous incline. From the hills behind Folkestone there was always white steam to be spotted somewhere in the vicinity of the Junction station, whilst a stupendous panorama could be obtained of the railway sweeping across the Pent valley and way beyond to distant Cheriton. The arrival of a train from the harbour was an unforgettable experience for any youngster who happened to be waiting at the Junction station. Across the many lines of the goods yard, the panting and echoing of the locomotives' exhaust could be heard long before they were seen, finally arriving at the exchange sidings where the 'R' tanks uncoupled and came off.

The visiting high society invariably came to Folkestone by train since the age of the motor car and charabanc was largely in its infancy. However, the needs of road vehicles were gradually having to be addressed as some of the bridges beneath the old SER main line were much too narrow. The first to be removed in Folkestone was Cheriton Arch, near the Central station, which was replaced in the early 1890s with an up-to-date steel girder span bridge. Gradually, the roads around Folkestone were improved but, as always, this served only to encourage motoring enthusiasts to travel faster. In September 1905, Sir Arthur Conan Doyle, who resided at Crowborough in Sussex, pleaded guilty through his solicitor to driving at 26 miles an hour along Cheriton Road. Since he'd already been convicted of a similar offence at Guildford, the famous writer was fined a somewhat hefty £10. Another gentleman who found himself at odds with the law was none other than Sir Alfred Watkin, who resided at 'Dunedin Lodge' in the West End. He refuted the charge of speeding, and claimed he was doing only 17 miles per hour, but the Kent constabulary thought otherwise and produced evidence from a device described as an 'electrical time measurer'. To no avail, Sir Alfred insisted that he was the best judge of speed since he'd not only acted as a fireman, but had driven railway locomotives hundreds of miles both in America and England. His protests made no difference and there followed a fine of £5 with costs.

Railway travellers were, of course, free from the constrictions of laws governing speeds on the King's highways and were at liberty to sit back in ease and comfort, able to watch the English countryside simply fly past the compartment window. However, such a blissful state of affairs was somewhat dented with the arrival of new contraptions in the name of economy. These were the steam railcars, a small steam locomotive and carriage combined in one unit, which inflicted misery, so it appears, on countless passengers across the land. It was partly due to the increasing popularity and availability of motor cars and charabancs that they became a necessity, brought about through falling railway receipts and

This Edwardian postcard, franked in 1906, provides an interesting view across the inner harbour from the roof of the Custom House. It appears that the connections between the branch and the sidings on either side, including the rail access to the Stade, had been dismantled. A new signal box had also replaced the smaller one which can still be seen nearby. An improved and enlarged Royal Pavilion Hotel features on the left, whilst, forming a backdrop above the smoky haze of the town, is Cubitt's viaduct.

The original Harbour station with its overall roof was removed when work began on the massive new pier reconstruction at the dawn of the 1900s. The Harbour House and clock tower were also demolished in 1899, whilst this part of the station was entirely rebuilt to ease some of the tight curves leading onto the pier. Here, in this 1905 view, a workman was engaged on repairs to the wagon turntable which gave access to the carriage dock on the right. Wagons could also proceed along the South Quay to his immediate left. Even with this remodelling, the check rail on the up line indicates the tight curves which caused wheels to squeal when making their exit. A replacement starting signal can be seen under construction behind the Pears soap sign.   COLLECTION NORMAN WAKEMAN

Porters, railway policeman and other staff at the Harbour station posing for the photographer at 1.36 p.m., judging by the time on the handsome SER longcase clock. Only 'Monday Dec. 12' may be glimpsed on the newspaper billboard poster; however, it also mentions President Roosevelt which therefore determines the year as 1904. The bookstall sold newspapers, postcards and journals, whilst a fine array of familiar advertisements of the period adorned the walls. The new gas lamp standard immediately in front of the camera was one of a row in the course of installation, whilst the canopy valancing was so typically South Eastern.

This view shows one of the fleet of coastal cargo freighters moored alongside the South Quay at high tide, and another ship moored in the repair yard. The twin-funnelled cross-channel was waiting to depart further out on the harbour arm which was unaffected by the variation in tides.

Below: An animated scene from 1905 depicting completion work under way on the massive new pier which came into use during 1904. The raised pier promenade is seen crowded with visitors who were able to walk out to the lighthouse. This view features the paddle steamer Duchess of York, built by R & H Green for the SER in 1895, alongside the pier, and, approaching, the LC&DR's Empress, built by Fairfield in 1887. A cargo steamer is just visible, hidden behind the rail-mounted travelling crane, whilst No. 302, one of the curious crane locomotives built by Neilson in 1881, features attached to a van in the centre.

COLLECTION NORMAN WAKEMAN

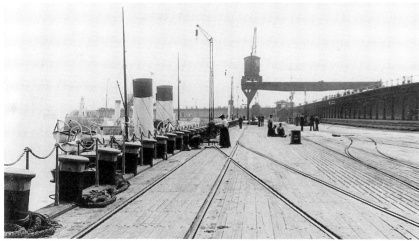

A view along the new pier of 1904 with one of the overhead travelling cranes in the background. COLLECTION NORMAN WAKEMAN

Container traffic is no modern innovation as witnessed here in this view of a beautifully maintained 'R' class No. 153 engaged in unloading and shunting duties in 1905. COLLECTION NORMAN WAKEMAN

This view from the lighthouse shows Empress, *the reconstructed harbour pier and the pier promenade thronged with visitors and sightseers.* COLLECTION NORMAN WAKEMAN

With ships on both sides of the harbour arm, the amount of activity can be well appreciated in this fine Edwardian view. Next to the locomotive blowing off steam we can see the SE&CR's new turbine steamer Onward, crowded with people and ready to depart. The SER's imposing Custom House in the foreground, with the elaborate SER coats-of-arms above the portals, was largely destroyed by shells during the Second World War. The landing stage on the outer side of the pier was used only when calm conditions prevailed. The tortuous 'S' curves in the railway may be appreciated.

COLLECTION ALAN TAYLOR

BOULOGNE BOAT, PREPARING TO START.

The SE&CR's Onward *(named after the motto on the SER's coat-of-arms) was built by Denny Bros. in 1905. These marvellous animated views show this powerful and well-liked ship being loaded and made ready for another crossing to France during those peaceful years before the Great War broke out. The motor cars were obviously the prize possession of keen enthusiasts who were perhaps touring down to Monte Carlo. Following* Onward's *diastrous fire and scuttling in 1918 during her time as a troopship, she was salvaged and repaired, before being sold and entering service with the Isle of Man Steam Packet Co. as* Mona's Isle.

No 34 THE HARBOUR.

The foreground of this view shows the cargo ship Folkestone nudging the quayside, but the attention is drawn to the new turbine steamer The Queen, with engines thrusting hard away given the amount of smoke pouring forth from the funnels. Built by Denny Bros. in 1903, The Queen proved herself in terms of speed and comfort, becoming immensely popular with the SE&CR's patrons. Historian Rixon Bucknall once described these particular steamers as 'Atlantic liners in miniature'. Regrettably, this beautiful ship was shelled by the enemy in 1916, before sinking beneath the waves of the English Channel just off the Varne bank.

FOLKESTONE.

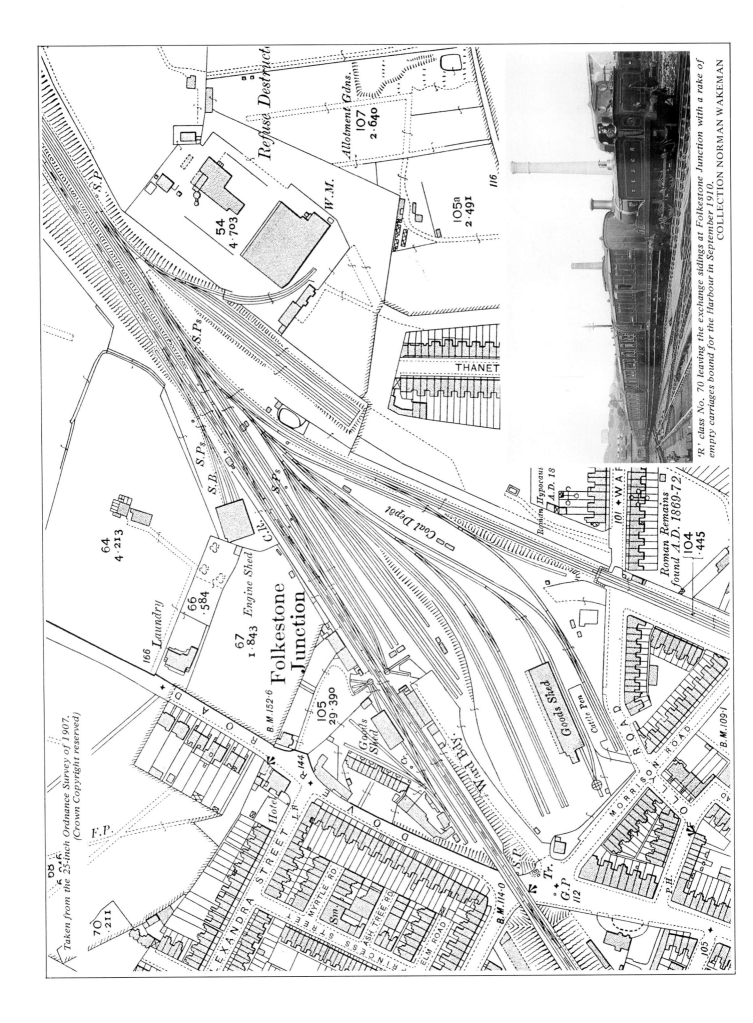

Taken from the 25-inch Ordnance Survey of 1907.
(Crown Copyright reserved)

Refuse Destructor

Allotment Gdns.
107
2·640

116

105a
2·491

THANET

54
4·703
W.M.

S.P.

S.Ps

S.Ps

S.B.

S.Ps

C.R.

S.Ps

64
4·213

66
·584

67
1·843 Engine Shed

166 Laundry

Folkestone
Junction

B.M.152·6

105
29·390

·144

Coal Depot

Goods Shed

W. and B.Ry.

Hotel

ALEXANDRA STREET

PRINCESS

MYRTLE RD.

Sm.

ASH TREE RD.

ELM ROAD

F.P.

70
211

70
211

B.M.114·0

S.P.

G.P.
112

Tr.

Roman Hypocaust
A.D. 18

Roman Remains
found A.D. 1869-72.

101 W.A.F.

104
·445

MORRISON ROAD

ROAD

B.M.109·1

P.H.

105

Goods Shed

Cattle Pen

'R' class No. 70 leaving the exchange sidings at Folkestone Junction with a rake of
empty carriages bound for the Harbour in September 1910.
COLLECTION NORMAN WAKEMAN

WARREN FOLKESTONE

A watchman standing in the doorway of his hut beneath the iron footbridge where, in 1908, the Warren Halt was constructed and opened to the public.

A 'B' class pounding through the newly-constructed Warren Halt at the head of a train bound for Dover.

a need for economy. Some of the local Folkestone services were eventually deemed suitable for the railmotors, although they were generally used only in the summer months to augment the ordinary services. Partly to coincide with their introduction, the SE&CR opened two new halts. The first of these was at Cheriton, brought into use in May 1908 and built on the Folkestone side of the embankment where the railway crosses Risborough Lane. It was barely half a mile west of Shorncliffe and, although served only by the Elham Valley trains, it proved popular with Cheriton folk who were able to buy their tickets from the lad at the little booking hut and board the services into Folkestone and beyond. It was also especially useful for taking trips into the Elham Valley and on to Canterbury for the popular weekly Market Day.

Exactly a month later, on 1st June 1908, the SE&CR opened the Warren Halt, likewise served only by the Elham Valley trains which continued through to Dover Town station. Remarkably, the original plans depict proper buildings on the up, or seaward side, with station offices, etc., but these were never constructed which was probably just as well given the events to come. Initially a weekday service of eight 'up' and seven 'down' trains were provided, with five each way on Sundays.

Following the arrival of the railmotors, the SE&CR began using them on the Dover Town-Sandgate service, whilst a similar short trip was instigated between Folkestone Junction and Elham where they terminated. They were unpopular with the public, though, whilst the most common complaint

The panorama from Grace Hill above the smoking chimney pots of Foord valley. Cubitt's magnificent 19-arch viaduct steals the scene, straddling the clustered terraces, back yards and lines of washing.

An 'F1' 4–4–0 leaving Folkestone Central station across the steel girder bridge of 1894 which replaced the original narrow brick arch. The motor age had finally arrived to challenge the supremacy of the railways, as witnessed by this Tilling Stevens omnibus.

levelled against them was their uncomfortable riding, caused through oscillation, which also made them very noisy. Their appearance on the railways around Folkestone was relatively brief, lasting for just six or seven years. These rather odd-looking and diminutive machines were positively dwarfed by the magnificent and breathtaking scenery of the Warren, which could make even the longest and grandest expresses appear little more than a toy train when viewed from such dizzy heights. From these cliffs the passing stroller, or those enjoying refreshments at Capel's wonderful clifftop café, may still watch a train emerge from Abbot's Cliff tunnel and run all the way through this marvellous terrain until swallowed up within the gloom of Martello tunnel. How insignificant the railmotors must have looked and how equally dwarfed they must have been by Cubitt's massive viaduct as they trundled across the span of this wide valley.

During 1913 another of the original narrow brick railway arches, dating from the early 1840s, was demolished to make way for road widening. This was adjacent to Cheriton Halt where the railway crossed Risborough Lane. Messrs Eastwood, Swingle & Co. provided a modern steel span which was erected on new brick piers before the old arch beneath was knocked down.

The somewhat idyllic days of those last few peaceful summers before the outbreak of the Great War became even more wistful in people's memories after 1914. The world really did change after that fateful Tuesday in August when war was finally declared on Germany and there could be no going back after the horrors of the ensuing years were eventually brought to an end. The effect upon Folkestone seems to have been almost immediate. The once-exclusive hotels of the Leas became deserted, whilst the flow of panicking German nationals returning to their home country was stopped and reservists arrested. Fleeing Belgians flocked across the channel whereupon the SE&CR laid on 'refugee

specials' from the Harbour station as and when required. Most departed around two o'clock in the afternoon, carrying around 300 souls at a time and running to London's Holborn Viaduct terminus. Stock from the Harbour sidings was used to convey these people who had fled their homeland in a frantic and desperate search for safety.

Gradually, the hotels and boarding houses of Folkestone were filled with soldiers billeted to the town before departure via the steamships to France and Belgium. Troop specials were run to special timetables, many calling at Westenhanger station on the way to pick up or set down men from nearby Lympne Camp. Ambulance trains were, of course, another regular feature, especially as the months rolled by and the alarming numbers of casualties so fearfully mounted. Many Red Cross specials transported men from Folkestone Harbour to the Kent & Canterbury Hospital which was conveniently served by the nearby Canterbury South station on the Elham Valley Line.

Perhaps the Elham Valley Line went some way to justifying its construction costs during the Great War when it was used as a diversionary route. Further use was made of the branch with the opening of the Canterbury loop line in 1918 which allowed running between the old LC&DR and SER lines - effectively creating a direct Canterbury West-London (Victoria) line. Nevertheless, its presence was undoubtedly seen as a blessing when, on the night of 19th December 1915, the Warren suffered the worst landslide in living memory. In fact, it was far more than a landslide, and equalled an earthquake since the damage was so severe and extensive. Francis Dent, for the SE&CR, flatly refused to comment on the future of the line, so great was the extent and magnitude of this natural disaster.

The events on that particular Sunday night were certainly dramatic, whilst the night watchman, who came on duty that afternoon at Folkestone Junction, could not have known

The fearful event of December 1915 is dramatically captured here, showing the alarming extent to which the land simply subsided beneath the train bound for Dover. The up distant signal for Folkestone Junction is seen tilted at a precarious angle, its arm erroneously showing 'all clear' by the chalk fall on its wire.
BRITISH RAILWAYS

Hawsers attached to the rear carriages of the ill-fated Dover service were used to salvage the derailed train.   LENS OF SUTTON

what he was about to experience. Shortly after a goods train had come through from Dover at around six o'clock, watchman Stockwell lit the wick of his handlamp and began walking towards Martello tunnel. On emerging into the Warren he detected some slight subsidence whereupon, just moments later, the ground began to tremble as a low, rumbling sound echoed in the darkness further along the line from the Dover direction. Instantly realizing what was happening, he hurried down to a sentry post at the seashore where a group of soldiers was standing outside in the partial moonlight, trying desperately to see what was taking place. Panting, Stockwell blurted out that he needed immediate assistance as a train was due to pass through very soon. By now the sound of falling cliffs and trees was clearly audible as huge sections began slipping, bringing many thousands of tons of chalk and earth thundering down.

Meanwhile, 'D' class 4-4-0 No. 493 in charge of the 6.10pm Ashford-Dover train was already on its way, having left the Junction station shortly after a quarter to seven. On board were around 130 passengers, mostly soldiers and sailors bound for Dover Harbour. Thankfully, it was running a little behind time, although Stockwell was too late to stop its departure when he rang through to the signalman on the trackside circuit. By this time the sentries, on Stockwell's instructions, had frantically tied red flags around some oil lamps, whereupon they headed towards Martello tunnel as fast as they could, waving the warning lights just as the train emerged. Fortunately an attentive driver saw them and immediately applied his brakes, slowing his train considerably. However, by the time he had brought his train to a complete standstill it stood close by the distant signal for Folkestone Junction, a few hundred yards on the Dover side of the tunnel. Before the train could be reversed out of harm's way, the ground beneath began to sink alarmingly, buckling the track and dragging down No. 493 and its coaches. Whilst the crew hurriedly 'dropped' their fire and made their engine as safe as they could, members of the armed forces quickly assisted all the other passengers out of the train and escorted them back on foot through the tunnel to the Junction station.

Further along the line towards Dover, the events of this cold, moonlit night were equally dramatic as this massive geological disturbance took place. At around 6.35pm platelayer Tom Down dashed into Abbot's Cliff signalbox shouting to signalman Wilding to 'stop all lines' as 'the cliffs are coming down'. Platelayer Down then left the box to see what else could be done, but ran back just seconds later, hollering to Wilding to 'clear out' quickly as the cutting behind his box was breaking up. Out into the moonlight, they both ran across the running lines, Wilding later telling the press: 'As I stepped on the rails I felt them go down quite a foot'. Joined by three soldiers who had fled from their nearby sentry, they all had to run for their lives as quite without warning an enormous section of the cliff suddenly came roaring and thundering down, engulfing the railway and carrying the little signalbox with it. Luckily, the

frightened men found their way to the footpath, which remarkably remained intact, so they were able to scramble to the top of the cliffs and safety. Here they dutifully set about hailing down motor traffic on the Dover-Folkestone road since large fissures were alarmingly opening up in the surface of the old coastal road.

While the railway was being entirely destroyed, Mr. and Mrs. Weston and their maid, who lived in a house appropriately named 'Eagle's Nest', were having an equally terrifying time. This handsome 'Tudoresque' residence constructed by Mr. Weston, a local builder, stood on a high promontory about fifty feet from the summit of the cliffs in a sheltered position commanding a stupendous view of the whole Warren far below. Settling down by their hearthside, they were alerted by a groaning noise from beneath the floor, accompanied by the sound of splintering wood and falling plaster. Unable to open their jammed doors, they had to hurriedly clamber out of a window to make their way to safety. Moments later the house, complete with its entire

This intermediate cabin with its hand-painted SER name, 'Abbot's Cliff Signals', was a casualty of the great landslide.
FOLKESTONE PUBLIC LIBRARY

Distorted and broken, the railway track disappearing beneath tons of fallen chalk in this dismal scene at daylight near Abbot's Cliff.
FOLKESTONE PUBLIC LIBRARY

The original railway alignment remains in the cutting and shows the extent to which the Warren halt was elevated and heaved seawards on that night.   FOLKESTONE PUBLIC LIBRARY

As good as new. A 1920 view of the repaired railway through the Warren, looking towards Martello tunnel.   BRITISH RAILWAYS

garden, began to sink as the whole foreland descended a hundred feet into the Warren. Incredibly, the house remained virtually complete, looking almost as though it had purposely been built there. However, with the view gone and the nervous disposition of Mrs. Weston after that event, Mr. Weston dismantled his fine home and re-erected it many miles inland at the tiny village of Little Chart, near Ashford, where they renamed their home 'Sanctuary'.

The Dover signalmen were told by Folkestone Junction that the line was blocked, but at that time no one realized the enormity of the damage. Families on afternoon visits to their sons stationed at the barracks found themselves stranded, resulting in quite a commotion and rush for the 'buses. However, Dover locomotive depot was able to muster up a train to take them back to Folkestone, but of course it was a long way round, involving travelling via Deal, Minster, Canterbury West and Barham.

As dawn broke on the following morning, the scene of devastation was scarcely believeable. The entire Warren Halt had not only been elevated, but heaved several yards seaward, whilst the track on either side was grotesquely twisted and broken. Over 250 yards of cutting were filled with tons of chalk and debris to a depth of 30 feet, whilst it was evident that the entire railway would require major re-engineering. All around, the landscape had taken on a new and quite ghastly appearance, with ruddy-brown smears down the white chalk giving an eerie impression and creating an almost Martian-like vista. The seashore had changed too. Incredibly, the sea bed itself had risen in places, exposing large plateaux of gault and revealing hidden reefs which formed new lagoons.

The rescue of the stranded train took place a week later, to which a reporter from the *Folkestone Herald* was invited to inspect the damage and witness the event:

'Plunging into the gloom of the Martello tunnel, we presently emerged at the spot where the train was partly engulfed by the subsidence of the line and here a remarkable sight presented itself. The track just outside the Warren end of the tunnel has sunk some twenty feet and the hole has become filled with water to a depth of six or seven feet. The engine and two foremost coaches of the train had been got out safely on to the track on the far side, but the remaining two vehicles were tilted at a steep angle. The foremost of the two was partly submerged and the bogies of the two coaches were torn away from the body. The locomotive, No. 493, was quite uninjured by its rough experience and was got out under its own steam, though there was a little difficulty in getting it up the slope on to the level. The engine, having been extricated, was utilised to haul out two of the coaches that were uninjured.'

The SE&CR pasted up notices that the line would remain shut until further notice. Kent County Council closed the road at Capel as the cracks continued to widen, although no further heavy falls took place. All 'bus services between the two towns had to be run via Kearsney and the Alkham valley, but flooding of the road at Drellingore led to further difficulties. Elham Valley trains started and terminated at

Shorncliffe station, but were later sent on to Folkestone Junction which became a terminus for the duration. Extra use was made of the line via Elham, but there were understandable complaints from Dover when extra goods charges were made, brought about by the lengthier rail journeys. Thirty railway employees had to move house from Dover to Folkestone as a result of the landslip and subsequent line closure, whilst the SE&CR seriously considered building an entirely new line further inland.

There were no aerial bombardments on the railways around Folkestone during the Great War, but the date of Friday 25th May 1917 will long be remembered by the town. Earlier in the day a raid on London had taken place and on the return journey a bomb was dropped on Tontine Street at the peak of the early evening shopping hour. The injuries caused were utterly sickening and although reported in grim detail at the time, remain far too gruesome to be repeated here. It seems the enemy had been aiming for the 4.40pm Charing Cross to Folkestone express which was in the vicinity of the Foord viaduct at the time. Awards were subsequently made to the train crew who handled the attack with fortitude. Likewise, James Pilcher, in charge of the railway horse 'bus at the Junction station, was presented with ten shillings for controlling his horse after it panicked and bolted following the detonation.

A most dramatic occurrence took place at the harbour in September 1918 when the SE&CR's steamship *Onward* caught fire. The naval fire-fighters were unable to control the blaze, whereby the order was given to open the sea-cocks. Sinking gradually to the bottom of the harbour, the vessel listed to port, until coming to rest on its side. Such drastic action was taken partly to save installations on the quayside, whilst wagons of equipment had to be quickly hauled clear. Assisting in these efforts was a small 0-4-0 saddle tank, built by Manning, Wardle & Co. in 1881 and numbered 313 by the SE&CR. As *Onward* listed, a snapped mooring wire entangled itself around No. 313, thereby dragging it towards the edge of the quay. Fortunately, a quick-witted crew member managed to cut through the wire with a cold chisel, thus saving the little tank engine from being toppled into the sea.

The rescue operation commenced a few weeks later following preparations by divers. Compressed air was pumped into sealed chambers of the hull as the tide rose while four locomotives exerted a pull of three tons through heavy wires and blocks. The engines used were 'O's Nos. 171 and 254 and 'R's Nos. 152 and 336. The exercise was a remarkable success, whereby *Onward* eventually returned to service.

The end of the war could not have come sooner for the SE&CR which had contributed enormously throughout the conflict. The organising of troop trains, refugee specials, ammunitions and stores supplies, as well as maintaining a civilian service to enable life to carry on, was little short of a miracle. Even so, the strain had been very great indeed, especially as the SE&CR had lost almost 500 of its own men enlisted to fight in the battles across the channel. Very

Enjoying the Sunday afternoon sunshine on the cliff above the harbour. The expansive Royal Pavilion Hotel can be seen in the far distance whilst the tower of the parish church features just behind the towering residence named 'Shangri-La'.

gradually, people began to put their lives back together, but the loss in human terms was simply astounding and its effects would reach far beyond to touch those generations yet to come.

Life in Folkestone had also changed, although brave attempts were made to get back to normal as soon as possible, whilst steamers were once again to be seen swinging away from Folkestone bound for the French and Belgian ports. Vestiges of the gracious life enjoyed by the Edwardians soon slipped away. One of the first casualties was the Sandgate Hill Lift which had suffered considerably during the Great War through the resulting obliteration of the holiday trade. My great-grandfather, Richard 'Bumpy' Kedwell, who'd been gainfully employed for many years as a brakesman/conductor on the lift and had ridden countless miles on its ornate cars, locked up the Lower Station for the last time in July 1918. Left to rust away and fall derelict, this charming Victorian apparatus was eventually dismantled for scrap in 1923.

Another casualty was the delightful horse tramway belonging to the SE&CR and which had given so much pleasure to thousands of visitors to this sunny corner of Kent. This likewise saw its receipts plummet following the outbreak of war, until in 1921 it was decided, not unexpectedly, to cease operation. Thus, Folkestone lost two of its unusual railways at an early date.

Following the grouping of the railways in 1923, the new Southern Railway Company soon established its identity and whilst the pace of change at Folkestone was initially slow, many improvements were already being planned. Early on, the harbour retained much of the air of the old SE&CR and

had a captivating atmosphere since almost everywhere something of interest was usually taking place. Partly because Folkestone suffered from distinct operating disadvantages, being cramped, with awkward, sharp curves in the railway, as well as the steep incline, the wanderer in search of the unusual was more than rewarded. It wasn't needful to be a railway enthusiast to marvel at the spectacle of two, three, or sometimes four tank engines taking a boat train up to the Junction. Stirling's trustworthy 'R' class locomotives continued performing their important tasks, the Southern having Nos. 125, 126, 152 and 153 based at Folkestone Junction. Two others, Nos. 107 and 339, had received Wainwright 'H' class boilers when rebuilt into class 'R1' before the war. Passers-by stood in awe at the sight and sound of these trains and, when all this commotion was over, there was still plenty left to experience for Folkestone was easily one of the most interesting harbours on the south coast. Having a rugged terrain, the roving eye could seldom tire from looking around this marvellous backdrop of clifftop hotels, villas and, below, the huddled fishermen's cottages, public houses, seaside cafés and shops which lined its narrow streets. The industrious nature of the harbour was quite probably objectionable to the lover of nature and all things rural. Nevertheless, the quaysides possessed their own peculiar fascination and, whilst the scene contrasted so markedly with the picturesque hamlet of a century before, its busy guise remained quite captivating. The filthy colliers which arrived, unloaded and departed, the coastal freighters which surrendered crates from their holds, as well as the fishing smacks with their pungent catches, lent so much

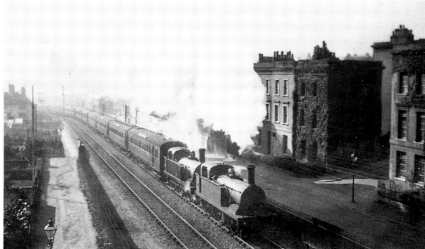

Great plumes of steam being ejected skywards from this pair of coupled tanks approaching the East Cliff or Radnor Bridge with a heavy train. G. A. STICKLER

'R' class No. 70 leading the branch train with steam to spare. Folly Road crossing keeper's cottage on the left was demolished in September 2002.

character to this part of the town. Some visitors shunned such workaday activity, preferring instead to remain in the West End where the once strictly-observed social barriers had, to a great extent, disappeared. The aspiring middle classes who now filled the boarding houses were generally content with the Leas, or patronizing the fashionable shops, exclusive restaurants and tea parlours of Sandgate Road, or strolling on the Victoria Pleasure Pier which graced the foreshore along the Lower Sandgate Road. However, so many could not help but be drawn to the old town, especially the harbour when the cross-channel steamers were arriving or departing. Here was a free spectacle, a chance to watch from the vantage point of the pier promenade the comings and goings of people from all walks of life. Writing in the *Railway Magazine* fifty

years ago, Henry Maxwell recalled those days after the Great War when Folkestone Harbour made such a lasting impression on him:

'It was the custom of the leading engine, whether of goods or boat train, when it received the right away, to signal 'cock-a-doodle-doo' on its whistle. This signal was repeated from the rear of the train - 'cock-a-doodle-doo' and then the train started. At all hours of the day, and even throughout the night at intervals, the wind would bear this 'cock-a-doodle-doo' upon its wings, and nothing entranced me more, when in my bed in the Pavilion Hotel by the inner harbour, than to hear this cheerful call and then to wait the few moments necessary for the purposeful exhaust of the engines to come into earshot, and the merry jangle of the wagons, with the distinctive resonance that they all

This snapshot taken in the mid-1920s captures 'R' class No. 155 banking a heavy train across the swing bridge at the foot of the incline towards Folkestone Junction. G. A. STICKLER

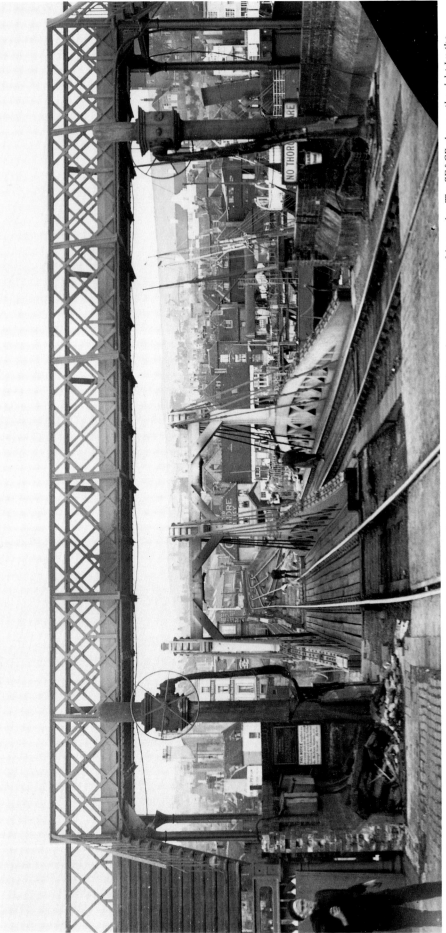

A 1921 glimpse across the swing-bridge, with a look-out standing by the up line holding a warning horn while workmen were engaged in repairs. The SE&CR sign on the right by the water crane states 'NO THOROUGHFARE', whilst the white board beneath the trespass notice near the water on the left crane warned 'This notice applies to everyone and only those who are engaged at work on the viaduct between the Fishmarket and the Harbour Station are exempt from it – By Order'.

The sharp curves through Folkestone Harbour station are well illustrated here in this view from September 1921. The break in the platform provided access to the West Beach carriage sidings. The turreted building was the pier promenade ticket office, whilst the adjacent building was Folkestone Harbour B signal box. The array of SE&CR pattern signals is impressive, whilst workmen engaged in renewing a section of the canopy valancing can be seen in the middle distance. Bilingual SE&CR signs, e.g. 'GENTLEMEN POUR LES HOMMES' provided a distinctly continental air.

The crew of 'R' class No. 70 posed with a young admirer in the down platform at Folkestone Harbour. The colourful array of railway posters is evidence of the desire to rebuild traffic after the recent war of 1914-18. G. A. STICKLER

This was the New Channel Station which was added in 1876. The iron footway led onto the promenade pier whilst the line trailing in from the right was the West Beach carriage siding.

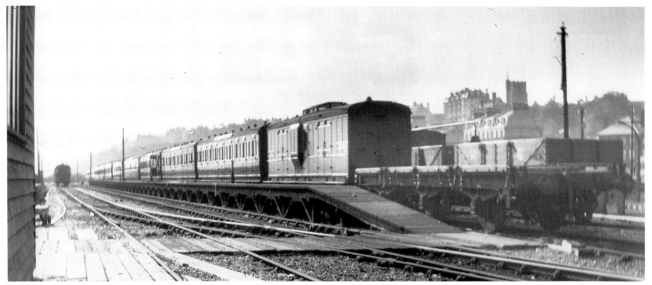

The extensive carriage sidings on the West Beach at Folkestone Harbour.

'R' class No. 153 in wartime SE&CR livery shunting on the pier.   COLLECTION PETER BAMFORD

A view from the footbridge of Folly Road crossing, looking towards Folkestone Junction, on 18th September 1925. Notice the catch points on the up line, the railwayman working in his allotment on the right, and beyond, the charabanc being attended to in the yard. F. J. AGAR

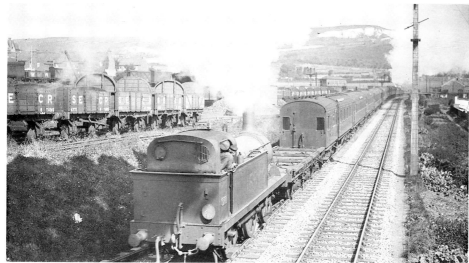

This view from the footbridge of Folly Road crossing shows 'R' class No. 155, in drab wartime livery, banking a London train up the branch on Friday, 18th September 1925. F. J. AGAR

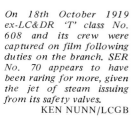

On 18th October 1919 ex-LC&DR 'T' class No. 608 and its crew were captured on film following duties on the branch. SER No. 70 appears to have been raring for more, given the jet of steam issuing from its safety valves. KEN NUNN/LCGB

No. 852 Sir Walter Raleigh starting away from the exchange sidings at Folkestone Junction with an up continental express bound for Charing Cross in the late 1920s. These beautiful locomotives were immensely powerful and admirably maintained the Southern Railway's crack express services throughout the South.
COLLECTION DENIS CULLUM

Folkestone Junction, looking towards Foord viaduct in 1922. The station was at one time the busiest in the town, not only with its passenger and goods business, but in having the Harbour branch and engine shed which is out of view to the right.

The railway into the Warren from the platform at Folkestone Junction in 1922. The signal box replaced the smaller one seen in previous pictures, whilst the soot-encrusted gantry controlled the main line and entry into the exchange sidings on the right. The Martello tower on the cliff was No. 1 of a whole line which once stretched as far as Seaford in Sussex.

'D' class No. 736, with a local train in tow, scuttling across the viaduct above Foord Road while everyone was enjoying the conviviality of a warm sunny day in the early 1920s.
COLLECTION R. C. RILEY

Gaslit Folkestone Central in early Southern Railway days. The standard SER signal box with its sash windows replaced the earlier structure (on page 29) while a set of 'birdcage' stock features in the bay opposite.

made as they passed on and off the swing bridge on their way up to the junction.'

By the late 'twenties there were visible changes to be seen everywhere. The four main stations of Folkestone were all painted in the smart dark green, buff and white of the new company, whilst a vivid and colourful array of posters covered the walls, advertising tempting holidays in Britain to places as far away as Scotland, Devon and Cornwall. Many of the express trains were beginning to be hauled by much larger and more powerful locomotives. The massive 'K' class 2-6-4 tanks, named after well-known rivers in the south, were truly beautiful engines which must have looked glorious in full flight with the Folkestone expresses. During 1927 a number were shedded at Dover and used for local services, presumably to test their mettle and capabilities. Nos. 800, *River Cray*, and 802, *River Cuckmere*, were seen running up and down the Elham Valley Line with Bank Holiday specials, although they were restricted to the branch speed of forty miles an hour. Tragically, only weeks later, with a trainload of people bound for Folkestone, Dover and Deal, *River Cray* jumped the rails at Sevenoaks and fell on its side, whilst the leading coaches smashed into an overbridge, killing 13 people and seriously injuring 43 passengers. Opinions differed as to whether it was the unsuitability of the permanent way rather than any intrinsic fault by the locomotive's designer Richard Maunsell. The entire class was withdrawn from service and eventually rebuilt with tenders which solved the problem of rolling at high speeds. Whether or not this was a public relations exercise to quell public anxiety remains a debatable point, but it did ruin the aesthetic appeal of a memorable and

A rare sight, caught in 1927, of the powerful new 'River' class at Folkestone Central.   G. A. STICKLER

admirable class of locomotive. However, there were other strikingly handsome engines to follow which were equally impressive and utterly breathtaking in their power and beauty. Unquestionably, to my mind at least, the Lord Nelson 4-6-0s in their original form were the loveliest of all to come from Maunsell's drawing board, a true mechanical genius of his time. Their power and great sense of majesty was simply awe-inspiring, almost frightening, whilst at speed there was nothing to equal the tingling thrill of the experience. These fine examples of British engineering made people's hearts swell with pride and every schoolboy watched in wonderment as these great machines glided past with such apparent ease. Graced with suitably impressive names, such as *Sir Richard Grenville*, *Howard of Effingham* and *Sir Walter Raleigh*, their gleaming presence on the trips to Folkestone surpassed even the heady days of the crack expresses of the old SE&CR. This, then, was yet another glorious era in the long and fascinating history of Folkestone's railways.

Whereas large passenger locomotives were to be seen on the viaduct high above the serried ranks of smoking chimney

'P' class No. 555 was a periodic visitor to Folkestone Harbour where it shunted the West Beach sidings or, as seen here, the quayside yard behind the goods warehouse.
G. A. STICKLER

Left: *Shunters and engine crew posing in the sunshine during duties.* Right: *The only known photograph of the SE&CR's Manning Wardle tank No. 752 in steam. Leaking somewhat, it was engaged shunting the quayside sidings.*
G. A. STICKLER

A most unusual visitor to the Harbour branch was 'O1' class No. 385 seen here banking a train in the early 1920s.   G. A. STICKLER

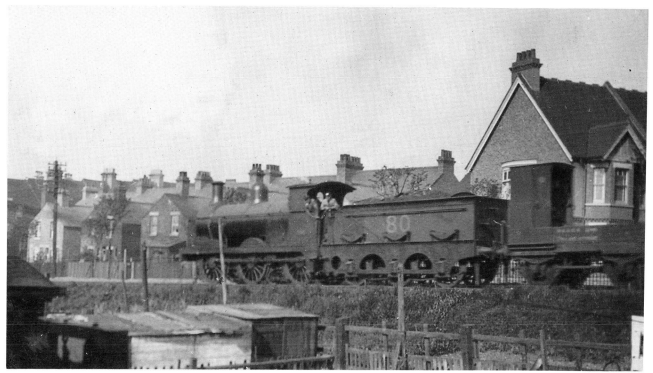

Another rare visitor was 'O1' class No. 80 captured here on the branch in this view of the early 1920s across the garden sheds near Folly Road Crossing.
G. A. STICKLER

pots of Bradstone Avenue and Foord Road, the Harbour branch steadfastly remained the preserve of the Stirling tanks. Occasionally, there were other interesting locomotives to be seen during the 1920s. Wainwright's smallest design, the neat and well-suited 'P' class 0-6-0 tanks, were regularly employed for shunting; Nos. 325 and 555 carrying on a tradition that seems to have been started with No. 27 during 1917. The SE&CR's only 'Terrier' No. 751 (ex-LB&SCR No. 54) also visited the quaysides here during the early part of the decade. Quite a variety of tank locomotives were tried on the Harbour branch, some suitable only for shunting, whilst others were used to assist in banking. One of the most successful trials involved an ex-LC&DR 'T' class 0-6-0T. Don Bradley relates that No. 609 had been sent here during 1899, proving itself more powerful than Stirling's 'R' tanks. However, there would have been no gain since two locomotives were still needed, thus it was sent back to Dover. Nevertheless, a 'T' class returned on at least one occasion when No. 608 was photographed here in October 1919. The real rarities were tender locomotives, but they were not entirely unknown over the branch and at least two of Stirling's rebuilt 'O1's were captured on film while working trains. No. 385 not only assisted with a train for Folkestone Junction, but No. 80, on another occasion, banked tender-first. Perhaps the most unique engine, however, was No. 752, built by Manning, Wardle & Co. in 1879. This diminutive locomotive had an interesting career, arriving at Folkestone Harbour in 1905 where it replaced crane tank No. 302 and remaining here until the outbreak of the Great War. For the

duration, it was exchanged with Tonbridge loco depot for another 'R' tank, No. 342, but enjoyed further adventures by being sent to shunt the yard at Hawkhurst in the Weald of Kent during hop-picking time. Affectionately nicknamed 'Thumper' by the crews, due to the noise it made at speeds more than 8 miles an hour, No. 752 eventually returned to Folkestone for a further few years until the summer of 1925 when a decision was taken to cut it up. However, 'Thumper' managed to escape this appointment with the scrapyard and was sold off instead to other owners. Happily, it found useful work for another eighteen years until, at last, its time came to be taken apart, melted down and its metal used for something else. Thankfully, though, its exploits at Folkestone were captured on celluloid, thus ensuring, in one sense at least, its immortality in historical books and among railway enthusiasts.

Many of the Stirling 'R's and 'R1's may well have gone the same way, some thirty years before their eventual departure. During 1929 the SR made plans to use a new design of locomotive, class 'Z' 0-8-0s which, it was anticipated, would do the work of two, perhaps even three, of the old SER tanks. However, since the 'Z's were far heavier than the Stirling 0-6-0s, the swingbridge of 1893 required complete rebuilding. Evidently the bridge was already classified as weak, since a working timetable of 1917 contains a note that only one line should be used at a time, or while shunting. Subsequently, during the weekend of 10th/11th May 1930 a new steel bridge, costing £23,000 and weighing 275 tons, was moved into place. By all accounts it was a major operation,

On Tuesday, 31st December 1929, as the decade came to a close, a roving photographer captured this scene at Folkestone Harbour where heavy granite kerbstones were being unloaded onto a solid-tyred motor lorry (KE 2487). Of perhaps greater interest is the adjacent steam lorry (M4329) likewise involved in the task. COLLECTION ALAN TAYLOR

beginning after the departure of the 3.50pm boat on Saturday afternoon. Around 120 workmen were engaged, whilst all continental services were diverted to Dover. On the following Tuesday, at eight in the morning, engines were sent to run over the new steel spans on deflection tests. Whereas the bridge was successfully installed, the trial runs with the new 0-8-0 locomotives were nothing short of a dismal failure. It must have been a huge disappointment for the SR, as well as an expensive exercise, for it soon became evident that they would not perform as hoped. Thus James Stirling's

small but trustworthy tanks triumphantly returned, much to the probable delight of the South Eastern men who knew their engines personally and were able to obtain the maximum tractive effort from them.

The rapid social changes which were taking place in the country obviously affected the railways. Even though it was the smallest of the British railway companies, the SR had to its advantage the popular, sunny south coast resorts and thousands of people packed into trains at holiday weekends, as well as the annual break. Commuter traffic was also on the

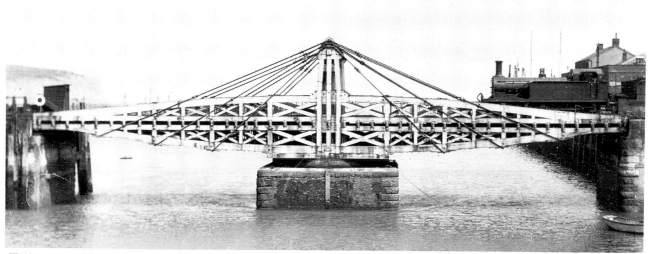

The last years of the wooden swingbridge, with 'R' class No. 153 at a stand on Saturday, 14th May 1927.　　H. C. CASSERLEY

One of Maunsell's 'Z' class 0-8-0Ts of 1929, No. 955, sandwiched between 'R' class No. 125 and 'P' class No. 323. The SR were hopeful of finding suitable replacements for the ageing 'R' and 'R1' engines, but the experiment failed miserably and the old Stirlings remained unchallenged for almost a further thirty years.
A. M. S. RUSSELL

A trio of 'R' tanks on shed near the turntable at Folkestone Junction which was officially a sub-shed of Dover.
H. C. CASSERLEY

Although in 1925 'R' No. 338 received its Southern livery, including prefix 'A' denoting Ashford, this locomotive, like many others, retained its cast 'SE&CR' cabside plate. Delivered to the SER in June 1888, it lasted until scrapping in March 1934. H. C. CASSERLEY

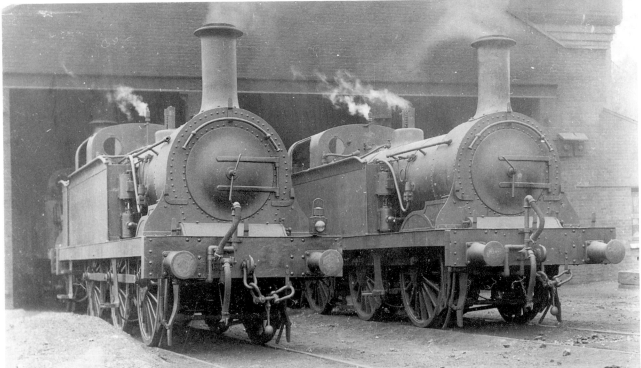

A pair of 'R's, Nos. 342 and 153, simmering quietly outside the engine shed at Folkestone Junction on Saturday, 14th May 1927.
H. C. CASSERLEY

There was always something to see at Folkestone Junction which remained a hive of activity throughout the day. A glimpse of this busy life is captured here in this view from the footbridge showing an 'R' tank which was in the course of shunting a London express in conjunction with the waiting 'Lord Nelson'. Among the delightful array of posters is one advertising the picturesque Wealdon town of Tenterden on the quiet backwater of the Kent & East Sussex Railway. H. J. STRETTON WARD

A pristine 'Lord Nelson' class, No. 853 Sir Richard Grenville, heading out of the exchange sidings at Folkestone Junction with a London express in the 1930s.
G. A. STICKLER

ascendent, but Folkestone was generally sustained by continental receipts, leisure travel and a healthy freight business. Even so, economies in working were being sought throughout the system, a process which had begun as early as 1925 when the receipts of certain branch and secondary routes were scrutinized. The results of these findings were put into effect during 1931, much to the dismay of neighbouring Sandgate which found itself entirely lopped off the system. Hythe managed to survive, although Watkin's anticipated new route to the continent was reduced to a single track.

Revisions in signalling came with the reduction of track and operations following the introduction of single line working over most of the Elham Valley branch. Only Lyminge and Harbledown Junction signal boxes remained open, the other five station cabins being removed and sold off. Elsewhere in the area, Hythe and Sandling Junction

(No.2) boxes were abolished once the branch had been singled. Shorncliffe lost its No.2 box as from 22nd June 1930, all movements being transferred to the larger cabin at the London end of the station. On this date also, 'Folkestone Junction B Cabin' was similarly dispensed with; its four signals henceforth controlled from 'A Cabin'. For the record, 'B' was situated 234 yards away on the up side of the Dover end of Martello tunnel. It had been brought into use only a decade earlier, on 1st August 1919, to coincide with the re-opening of the railway through the Warren. Incidentally, the small wooden cabin seen in early photographs of Folkestone Junction station was replaced in November 1908 by the much larger structure built on a brick base. At Folkestone Central the only change came when the original Cheriton Arch cabin was replaced with the more-familiar SER box, assumed to have been brought into use with the provision of

No. 865 Sir John Hawkins working an up boat train from Dover, to the admiration of strollers making their way to the tea chalet in the Warren, in the balmy days prior to the Second World War.
NATIONAL RAILWAY MUSEUM

the 'up' bay road in 1896. At Folkestone Harbour there were at one time three signal boxes, 'A', 'B' and 'C', to control the somewhat complicated movements dictated by the rather awkward layout. 'A' box was always very conspicuous, being perched above the low viaduct across the Inner Harbour. Originally there was only a small cabin here, used to control facing connections, but it was eventually replaced with a standard SER 'clapboard' affair, distinctive in postcards of the day. The next signal cabin, 'B', was situated at the seaward end of the up platform, where the carriage sidings on the west beach diverged. Finally, 'C' box stood on the pier itself. In September 1922 both 'A' and 'C' were abolished, leaving only the cabin situated on the platform controlling all movements. Eventually, this structure was superseded by the more modern and larger affair erected near the swing bridge and which survives to this day. The SR obtained a secondhand Saxby cabin for this purpose, quite likely one made redundant from the Brighton line resignalling and brought this into use during December 1933.

Apart from recollections of Sunday School treats to Lyminge and Barham, my father recalls events which took place some years later. Some of his friends would occasionally wander up to the railway line near the gasholders at Foord where a platelayers' hut made a convenient rendezvous. Safe from parental gaze, they were able to attempt smoking cigarettes, but a look-out was always necessary in case of routine track gangs. It was also very needful to keep a sharp eye on the signals, all of which were easily visible. He remembers the up starting signal at Folkestone Junction, which was a very tall bracketed affair dating from SE&CR days, whilst the down stop signals had three arms in a row, one for the Dover line and two for the Harbour branch sidings. If the arms of these dropped forty-five degrees, then it was time to hide from the vigilant eye of the passing train crews. On one occasion, the civil engineers had been carrying out repair work to the brick arching of Foord viaduct, a pit having been dug down through the 'four foot' from above. A foolhardy dare involved my father crouching into this pit where he was to remain while a train passed overhead. He can still remember his pounding heart, the roar of the train and the glow of the firebox - a thoroughly frightening experience and one which afterwards he had absolutely no desire ever to repeat.

Rough seas are fairly commonplace during the winter months at Folkestone when huge waves roll in before thumping against the harbour pier. The might of the sea during severe storms is both exciting and terrifying, whilst it is a wonder that the harbour has withstood the pounding whereas other coastal defences are entirely washed away. Railway staff and fishermen are used to seeing breakers crash over the pier, but freak weather conditions have sent tidal waves which have brought death in their wake. One such incident occurred in 1812 when Folkestone was just a small fishing town, whilst the last in living memory took place in mid-summer, on Saturday, 20th July 1929. The event illustrates how suddenly these events can happen and involved my mother, just seven years of age, who was out walking with her father along the promenade. An increasingly darkening sky heralded a strong wind which blew up the English Channel, driving before it a huge swell. As this approached Folkestone, a mountain of water swept inland without warning, surging up the beach and even breaking over the railway pier. The wave engulfed them both and my mother was saved only by the quick-witted actions of her father who used his walking stick to hook her to safety. Less fortunate was a 16 year-old lad, Arthur Balkham, quietly fishing at Copt Point at East Wear Bay, who was lifted off the rocks by the sudden incoming swell and swept out to sea.

Apart from natural incidents, there have always been instances of human folly, such as the time in 1937 when a passenger lingered too long in the Harbour station buffet, then dashed out just as the 'Golden Arrow' was leaving and foolishly attempted to board it. He managed to grab the handrail of a Pullman car, but slipped, his legs left dangling perilously beneath the platform where the curvature of the line created a gap between the platform and train. A railwayman, James Wilson, pluckily grabbed the man and pulled him away in the nick of time as moments later he would have been crushed where the clearance between train and platform was at its narrowest. The boat train, which just happened to have on board Sir Herbert Walker, the general manager of the SR, was brought to a stand, but restarted once the drama was over. In due course, Wilson was awarded with a gold watch and cheque for his courageous action.

Problems with the Warren manifested themselves again in 1939 when, after a spell of prolonged wet weather, chalk falls took place throughout the Folkestone area. Only five years earlier the SR had seriously considered building a 'by-pass' route, whereby a lengthy tunnel would be driven further inland from Folkestone Junction, beneath the cliffs at Capel and emerging on the Dover side of Abbot's Cliff. It seems the financial backing for this major exercise was to have formed part of a national government programme of economic recovery through capital spending on infrastructure.

During the 1930s Folkestone Junction shed had retained six Stirling tanks, three of the last remaining 'R's, Nos. 1070, 1125 and 1153, as well as three 'R1's - 1107, 1128 and 1340. By 1939, however, the unrebuilt engines had been replaced with 'R1's, Nos. 1047, 1127, 1154, and included a seventh addition, No. 1337. Most were soon surplus to requirements whereby two, Nos. 1127 and 1128, were sent up to Headcorn for storage in the sidings where they were appreciably safer from bombardment.

Following the declaration of war on Germany in September 1939, and the eventual fall of Belgium and France, the railways of Folkestone were once again thrust quite literally into the firing line. This time there was not only the threat of enemy attack, but a very real prospect of invasion by Hitler's forces. Numerous defences were installed all along the south coast using barbed wire and tank traps. My father remembers the swing bridge being positioned so as to make it impassable for both trains and vessels, whilst concrete was poured into its machinery. Not unexpectedly the town suffered severe bombing, the railway, harbour and Foord

This aerial view of the viaduct, looking west in May 1949, shows how the town and industry of Folkestone grew in the century following the arrival of the railway. The gasholder in the foreground was the one ruptured by enemy attack during the Second World War.
COLLECTION ALAN TAYLOR

viaduct being obvious targets. Hythe station received a direct hit which destroyed the parcels office, but incredibly both Shorncliffe and the Central stations escaped unscathed. A number of high explosive bombs fell near the Junction station, but damage was limited to nearby houses. However, 'Jerry' had better luck at the harbour where a shell blew out the track at the station, whilst another almost destroyed one of the arches near the swing bridge. Perhaps the greatest loss was the fine Customs House, dating from SER days. This lovely building was wrecked, whilst heavy and concentrated pounding in the area obliterated large tracts of the most characterful and picturesque parts of the old town which both my parents fondly remember. Elsewhere, Cheriton Halt had a near miss when a high explosive bomb landed in Broomfield Road, but since the halt had been closed following the withdrawal of passenger services over the Elham Valley Line in December 1940, it would not have mattered much. Miraculously, Foord viaduct evaded destruction, although enemy guns on the French cliffs fired shells at it. The closest shave came when a high explosive shell actually passed through one of the arches before exploding in Bradstone Avenue. Another near miss involved a bomb which fell instead near No. 4 gas holder on the eastern side of Foord valley. Shrapnell from the blast punctured the steel casing of this gasometer, setting it on fire and allowing foul-smelling water from the base of the holder to gush out and flood into houses below.

Another casualty of the war in the railway sense was the Metropole Lift, opened in 1904 to serve the western end of the Leas. The military authorities thought it could be useful for allied troop movements following an enemy invasion. However, their recklessness and indifference in operating the water-balance lift led to the cars being allowed to run at such an uncontrollable speed that the cast-iron tanks and underframes were irreparably cracked on impact with the buffer rests. Thus the installation was economically ruined. After the war the Folkestone Lift Company deemed it too expensive to provide new cars, especially as claims for compensation against the military were hindered. As a result, the unfortunate Metropole Lift, incidentally the only one in Folkestone capable of conveying bathchairs, was subsequently dismantled for scrap.

In early 1944, when the liberation of Europe was being organized by the allies, extra trains and locomotives were sent to Folkestone. As with the earlier but disastrous Dunkirk campaign, the town stood in readiness, whilst the port was alive with military traffic and personnel. The 'R1's were yet again very much in evidence following wartime dispersal which had led to 1107 and 1154 being based at Tonbridge, 1047 and 1340 at Ashford, with 1337 held over at Dover. These, together with the two previously in store at Headcorn, were re-allocated to Folkestone which was a sub-shed of Dover.

Soon after the war there came further changes. The townsfolk sought the restoration of the train service to Canterbury and, whilst the Hythe branch was revived, the Elham Valley Line saw passenger trains running only as far as Lyminge. However, there was hope in the wind when the local press gave details of the electrification programme which the SR intended resuming. This promised to have electric trains running to Folkestone by the end of 1949 with the Elham Valley Line and Hythe branches being worked by diesel engines. Thus, so it appeared at that time, steam trains would soon be a memory. However, the course of history is never smooth and rarely follows such high hopes and aspirations.

In June 1947 the SR decided instead to withdraw all traffic from the Elham Valley branch, thus ending almost sixty years direct rail connection between the town and the city of Canterbury. Four years later, in 1951, it was the turn of the Hythe branch to be removed from the railway map since road transport and a comprehensive 'bus service had taken away virtually all its business. Folkestone also lost two of its halts. Cheriton had enjoyed a brief re-opening after the war with the resumption of the Lyminge service, but few people used it, whilst the Warren Halt lasted rather longer, even though trains had not been scheduled to regularly stop there for some years. Its final entry in the timetables seems to have been the winter edition of 1953, for in the following year it was deleted. Nobody bothered to use it, whilst the trains henceforth rattled straight through, although it was still possible to alight there by requesting the train crew to stop.

My family's regular summertime excursions into the Warren were normally made by East Kent 'bus to Wear Bay Road and from there they would tramp down the white, dusty chalk paths on foot. However, to ring the changes, my father decided one Sunday to visit instead the deserted beach beyond Abbot's Cliff. Although I was much too young at the time to remember this particular adventure, my father relates what happened:

'Thinking back to that train ride to Shakespeare Halt, I recall that my initial enquiry at the booking office was met with the suggestion that I asked the driver of the slow train which was languishing at the down platform in readiness for its noon departure, after the express had passed through. This I did, but the driver referred me to the guard for he said it would be up to him

The small, staff-only halt at the foot of the Dover cliffs.

One of Bulleid's new 'West Country' locomotives, No. 21C134 (later named Honiton) running through Folkestone Junction with a Dover–London express in the late 1940s.

H. C. CASSERLEY

whether or not to apply the brakes, which seems a bit strange now, but I'm pretty sure that's what I was told. The guard gave his blessing to the idea, for I guess the challenge of halting the train with our compartment alongside the short railway-sleepered platform would have added a bit of 'zip' to his otherwise routine shift. However, he had to point out that his tour of duty ended at the Junction station, but he promised to pass on the message to his relief. Understandably then, we were just a little apprehensive as the train rattled somewhat hastily through the final stretch of Abbot's Cliff tunnel with no hint of any brakes being applied, although our worries proved to be premature, for then, almost at once, we were aware of the rapid decelleration of the train to the loud squeal of the brakes, whereupon our carriage door faced out squarely on the aforesaid platform. Our alighting was witnessed by passengers all along the train, who could have been forgiven for expecting to see someone of V.I.P. status disembarking at this unscheduled port of call. The wooden platform abutted the awesome chalk cliff face towering above us and prompted thoughts of the wartime cliff fall of some 45,000 tons in that region.'

No doubt those who'd popped their heads out of compartment windows to see why the train had stopped at such an insignificant place wondered who on earth could ever wish to alight in the middle of nowhere. As the last carriage was swallowed up within the nearby murky blackness of Shakespeare tunnel, my father recalls it was a very risky business crossing the line, requiring extreme care and attention as 'up' trains dashed out of the imposing, but hugely daunting, Gothic portal with little warning. He also recalls that day seeing the:

'....German M.E.110 twin-engined fighter bomber, the wreck of which slowly manifested itself on the rocks as the tide gradually receded. Facing in the direction of Dover, with its propellors badly buckled, it remained marooned there for quite some years as a silent but grim reminder of those earlier dark days of the 1940s.'

Having had the entire beach to themselves that day, the problem of getting home in the late afternoon loomed every bit as large as Shakespeare Cliff which stood between them and the railway station in Dover. There seemed no chance of boarding a train home until a kindly railway workman, who lived in one of the old colliery cottages close by, thought he

'Battle of Britain' class No. 21C154 Lord Beaverbrook *snaking out of the exchange sidings with the Victoria-bound 'Golden Arrow'. Throughout the next decade the Bulleid Pacifics would handle all the SR's crack expresses to the channel ports.*

The Folkestone Warren sweeping round towards Abbot's Cliff and onward to Dover. This is the view from the bridge near 'Little Switzerland'. Below is the railway emerging from Martello tunnel next to the adjacent cinder trackway which led on down to the foreshore where in the 1950s so many happy Sundays were spent.
E. R. HART

might be able to help. Ringing through to Dover Priory signalbox on the railway circuit, he managed to arrange for the next 'up local' to make an unscheduled stop, and thus they were gratefully taken back home to Shorncliffe.

On another occasion, when I was just a toddler, a bright, hot, sunny day had given way by early afternoon to an increasingly darkening sky as leaden storm clouds menacingly loomed over the cliffs. Having hurriedly packed up, my parents headed back up the cinder path towards the railway where my father noticed a train pulling into the Warren Halt to pick up some workmen. My mother was reluctant to attempt boarding the train, whereas my father was adamant we weren't going to risk it as booming rumbles of thunder and great arcs of lightning heralded an imminent downpour. British Railways obligingly came to the rescue whereby, quickly settling my sister, myself and themselves in a compartment, the train soon restarted, sparing us a thorough drenching. Unsure that the train would stop at Shorncliffe, my parents alighted at Folkestone Central where my father asked at the booking office grille for: "Two and two halves from the Warren Halt". For a moment the clerk looked somewhat perplexed, scratched his head, then reached up to a high shelf where he brought down an old ledger from which he blew a huge cloud of dust! Thumbing through the stained and yellowed pages he scoured the long lists of fare tables before finally giving up, saying: "Oh, - give us a 'bob'."

The railway through the Warren and this most spectacular of English landscapes made a substantial impression on my early memory. In many ways I have good reason to be thankful that very few families in the 'fifties had the money to lavish on the kind of entertainment and days out which nowadays cost a small fortune. Nor can I help wondering whether today's youngsters will be able to look back and draw upon their childhood memories with such deep affection and warmth. The summer of 1959 turned out to be extraordinarily fine and settled, so much so, that even today my aunt Doris wistfully recalls those thirteen consecutive happy weekends we were able to spend there. Picnics, which included such simple favourites as squashy tomato or ripe banana sandwiches, cold boiled potatoes, hard-boiled eggs and home-made fruitcake, were packed into old biscuit tins along with the kettle and Dad's reliable, polished-brass blowlamp for making tea. Methylated spirit was put in the trough at the top in order to heat the vapourizing pipe before the priming pump forced out the paraffin through the jet. It boiled a kettle within minutes, whilst there was always plenty of fresh water from the numerous springs which gushed out of headings driven into the chalk. Although there were green vitreous-enamel railway notices with the rather dire warning 'NOT DRINKING WATER', the taste of these natural springs was truly wonderful, however, and quite unlike the chemically-treated substance which nowadays we have to tolerate from our domestic taps.

We also took with us a few simple implements for entertainment. Gaily-painted metal buckets, wooden spades, miniature paper flags for sandcastles, a rubber ball and a cricket bat was really all that was required as aunties, uncles, cousins, grandparents and sometimes neighbours and their children boarded the No. 106 service to Hill Road. Having made its circuit through the steep hills of the town, the maroon and cream East Kent 'bus with its long bench seats on the upper deck, whined and bounced its way up Dover Road, passing beneath the skew arches, carrying us higher and higher to our destination. The walk along Wear Bay Road overlooked the Junction station where the sounds of expresses, freight and local trains came drifting up, as well as the 'R1's in glorious concert on the Harbour branch. Once past the very first of the old Martello towers, which in those days was a grim, dark and rather fearsome ruin, we'd catch our first glimpse of the glinting steel lines of the railway

stretching through the Warren towards Dover. The dry chalk paths and private road which led down into the Warren ran close to the main line and the Dover end of Martello tunnel. At its entrance stood the up home signal for Folkestone Junction and there I'd linger, hoping its arm would soon rise skywards. I was rarely disappointed as, moments later, a flurry of steam beyond the Warren Halt would announce the arrival of the expected train which would come rushing along only to be swallowed up within this great dark cavern that appeared so daunting to a young mind. Great clouds of vapourising steam would continue wafting out for some time afterwards, whilst occasionally there'd be the echoing sound of an approaching express bound for Dover. Suddenly bursting out, its clatter and vibration would excite an already pounding heart as huge, glossy spoked wheels and glistening motion, which sweated oil and steam, raced in a blur as hissing pistons furiously drove clanking coupling rods. Whilst the roar from carriage wheels drowned our cheers, our frantic waving was almost always returned by the friendly

Above: *Family snapshots in the Warren. My parents enjoying the sunshine in one of the bays created by the new sea wall.* Top right: *Cousins Barbara, Avril, and sister Marion finding plenty of amusement in one of the many exposed rock-pools at low tide.* Right: *A young Brian Hart wondering whether he'll ever master the art of building sandcastles!*
E. R. HART

passengers peering expectantly from the windows of the gleaming green coaches.

Throughout those days, memories of which seem to be so full of images of bright sunshine and sparkling sea, we'd hear the trains at all times of the day. At low tide, venturing out among the rock pools and slipping upon wet patches of bluish gault, the view broadened out to Shakespeare Cliff, whilst from Abbot's Cliff a trail of steam would mark the presence of a train which would, within minutes, rumble through the cutting behind us. The sound of whistling locomotives very much filled the air throughout the day, causing me to pause from building my fortress of sand against the incoming tide, or rockpool exploration, and gaze towards the railway. Most of the background noise came from the sea, of course, where waves would be breaking further out, but by the time these reached my toes they would be smooth carpets of water which would trickle into the channels and moats I had dug. Tiny shrimps and crabs would scuttle around in the warm, gritty, saline pools, but this involvement was always superseded by interest in the railway. Whenever a train from Dover passed through, we'd see great white clouds of steam jetting out, accompanied by the muffled beat from the locomotive and its line of clattering carriages, the sound reverberating back from the surrounding cliffs.

In an effort to prevent further major slippages in the Warren, the Southern Region built a range of substantial concrete sea defences including a wall with ramps at right angles for added strength. These created bays which provided convenient places to settle for the day, as well as giving us shade from the often searing noonday sunshine. There was also a huge concrete apron which projected some distance into the sea at high tide, its end washed by waves, making the surface green, slippery and treacherous near the edge and engendering a fear of deep water. A variety of small wagons could be trundled along the narrow gauge lines embedded in concrete, whilst there were other tracks used in the sea defence works which were laid up the cliff face to the Warren sidings. Deserted wooden buildings gave it a mildly American West feel, especially when a gust of wind caused doors to creak on dry hinges or blew debris along the chalky, dusty tracks on which we played. Tarred shacks and derelict sheds, drainage headings into the cliff, as well as rusting, forsaken items of machinery, all seemed to be waiting there for our investigation whenever the fascination of the seashore had waned.

The comings and goings of the cross-channel ships to and from Folkestone harbour were less obvious from the Warren, although the graceful lines of some of the vessels were particularly appreciable from this distance, especially the ex-Southern Railway vessels *Canterbury* or sister ship *Isle of Thanet*. If anything caused me to drop my spade, it would be the sight of one of these ships suddenly appearing from behind the headland of Copt Point, steaming hard away from Folkestone and often trailing a cloud of heavy black smoke, leaning portside and swinging towards the open sea and Boulogne, Calais or Ostend. On the return trip from the

continent, the captain would swing his ship 180 degrees hard to starboard, before reversing into the harbour. This manœuvre often caused a wash some five minutes later, but never did any harm except for demolishing my sandcastles earlier than I'd anticipated. However, on one occasion an over-zealous turning in the offing caused a freak wave to surge into the Warren. I remember playing intently at the water's edge, not taking too much notice of the increase in wave activity until the audible drag of chattering pebbles became noticeably alarming. Looking behind me, I became rooted to the spot in astonishment as this huge wall of water suddenly appeared, whilst any attempt to escape would have been utterly futile. I recall how the top of the wave curled and began to break - the next moment I was aware of the strange sound of the sea from beneath the water and how amplified everything became. In this strange green world I found myself clutching at nothing as I, and seemingly all the stones on the beach, were dragged into the sea. Then, I felt my father's arms around me, lifting me up, spluttering and choking from the salt water up my nose and down my throat. In fact, the force of the wave had been so great that it had swept right up to the sea wall, engulfing everyone's belongings that day. I remember how a kindly stranger returned my gran's false teeth after a panic search! Happily, though, our days were normally without incident and for me were spent in blissful, innocent, contentment.

Towards the end of the afternoon the whole family would pack up belongings and head for the 'green'. This was a level and fairly large area of short grass only a few yards from the railway and just behind the Warren Halt, where we all enjoyed a game of rounders. A substantial wooden bridge once spanned the halt and my excitement would grow as the family dawdled up the black and dusty cinder track which led up to the railway from the seashore. Often I'd go on ahead and clamber up the steps of the grimy, buff-painted bridge, desperately hoping a train was due. Looking along the shimmering rails towards the Martello tunnel, I'd wait in hopeful expectation for the signal arms on either line to bounce skywards. Once this had happened, there was no chance of being coaxed away until the train had passed through. Trains for Dover would burst out of the tunnel, half a mile away, steam fizzling from side to side out of the indistinct shape in the distance. Gradually the roar would increase, the rails singing in harmony when all of a sudden the train was upon us, vibrating the planking of the bridge as an upsurge of hot air, steam, oil and smoke engulfed us, momentarily obscuring the view, before it disappeared round the curve and into the cutting towards Abbot's Cliff. In the opposite direction there was more excitement when the Folkestone Junction 'up' distant signal came 'off' - usually denoting a London express. These could be heard leaving Abbot's Cliff tunnel, pounding hard through the cuttings with a heavily-laden boat train, before thundering underneath with a shower of smuts flying all around.

The Warren was truly a place of great contrasts in all spectra of human senses. The sights and sounds were impressionable

A Bulleid Pacific in the new British Railways livery slipping across the viaduct above Foord Road with the down 'Golden Arrow'.

A. W. V. MACE

enough, but speaking for myself it was the range of smells which probably had the most impact upon my memory. Even today, I need only catch the slightest whiff of burning methylated spirit from a blowlamp, hot tar or creosote, a steam locomotive, or the scent from certain shrubs to be immediately reminded of those blissful times. Leaving behind the fresh tang of salt sea air and seaweed-strewn beaches, I became aware of the pungence of sweating tar which oozed from wooden railway sleepers after a blisteringly hot day. The lengths of shining steel rails stretched and creaked with the sun's heat which radiated back from the immaculately-tended permanent way but, within just a few steps, everything changed as the footbridge led directly into the greenery of the Warren. Standing on the wooden planking, the sound of surf breaking upon the shore and the trains incessantly coming and going occupied the mind. A moment later the bridge came to an end, where timber decking met the chalk paths which wandered off deep into the wilderness. The winding path which trailed towards the direction of Dover once led to a popular tea chalet, set up by some enterprising individual many years ago when excursionists alighted at the Warren Halt. What a joyful, if simple, outing this must have been for so many people in the early years of the twentieth century. My uncle Joe worked here for a time during the 1930s; however, once the halt lost its service and the war

came, the café closed and the surrounding undergrowth quickly reclaimed the site.

The other path led off towards the 'green' which to me seemed like a little patch of civilization amidst the barely penetrable jungle all around. Throughout our games here, the railway would never allow its presence to be forgotten as trains continued whistling and rumbling in the cutting below. Soon, the bright, summer sun would begin to sink behind the awesomely-high cliffs above East Wear Bay, whilst a cooling, late afternoon breeze would rise, welcomingly wafting across reddened, sunburnt limbs. The landscape of the Warren seemed at times almost tropical, especially to a young mind from a vantage point barely thirty inches from the ground. Thick bines, on which we'd attempt to swing, hung down from towering trees, whilst the wild clematis, or 'granddad's beard', ran completely amok. Bright green hart's-tongue ferns and other damp-loving plants thrived in the cool, shady interior where winding and steeply tortuous paths led off in all directions. The fear of basking adders also gave it a sense of danger, although only rarely have I seen these timid, much-maligned and misunderstood creatures there. If we were lucky we'd spot a lizard on a chalk outcrop, whereas butterflies seemed to be in abundance, gathering upon the lilac-coloured swathes of common buddleia blossoms. Little wonder that my great-grandfather, George

Millgate, who had a magnificent butterfly collection, loved venturing into the Warren on his days off. I remember, too, the heady sweetness of red valerian, but most of all the delicate scent of the tiny yellow vetch. When I was a little older I'd often clamber up the steps cut out of the chalk and strengthened with old railway sleepers and lengths of redundant rail, but as a toddler, I'd usually be carried on my father's shoulders. At the top of the steps we'd reach 'Little Switzerland', a convenient tea chalet which to this day still occupies a marvellous position, although often I'd be asleep by then, too tired even to watch the trains below as they ran through this most remarkable landscape in the county of Kent.

Very occasionally, we would spend a summer's afternoon upon the crowded sands at Folkestone, at the far eastern end of the Stade, where a grand view of the harbour and the cross-channel ships could be obtained. The departure of a vessel was always an event, a deep blast issuing forth from the whistle on the funnel as the propellers churned white foam around the stern. Their arrival on the horizon was also something to watch. Gradually growing in size, they began to swing round to starboard, causing quite a wash, before reversing in to dock.

On Sunday afternoon walks along Coolinge Lane to the Leas my father would show me where the Sandgate Hill Lift had once operated. Then we would either go down the zigzag path to the Lower Sandgate Road and the seashore, or further along the Leas to watch the quite unique twin installation of water-balance lifts. Usually, I would want to stay longer than H. G. Wells' character Kipps who would 'watch the lift up and down *twice*, but not longer, because that wouldn't do'. A treat would be a ride in the 1890 lift with its curious, stepped seating arrangement, then my parents would sometimes take me onto the harbour pier. Here I could see the enormous cranes which so dauntingly moved along their overhead gantries, loading and discharging from ships' holds. These green-painted metal giants would straddle the pathway along the pier's length, running along rails embedded in the granite stonework. From a little window in his wooden cabin high up on the gantry, I could see the craneman looking down, skilfully controlling his machinery, comprising levers, cables and little wheels which spun round very fast, entrancing many a small boy.

Activity below was equally absorbing where an 'R1' would be somewhere along the railway lines, marshalling trucks or carriages for the London boat train. The all-pervasive briny

'R1' No. 1047 *assisting in the business of the day on the pier head while coastal freighter* Maidstone *was being loaded.*

COLLECTION R. C. RILEY

The eastern end of Folkestone Harbour station showing the buildings dating from 1876. The elevated walkway on the right led to the pier promenade, for which tickets were required, and passed directly over the line which gave access to the West Beach sidings, hence the break in the platform.

COLLECTION DENIS CULLUM

A delightful moment captured as the locomotive crews were waiting at Folkestone Harbour before taking their train up the branch on Saturday, 17th September 1955.

J. H. ASTON

atmosphere intermingled delightfully with the aroma of steam, coal smoke and hot oil from the old Stirling tank engines which busily fussed around just a few feet below. Wooden decking interwoven with steel railway lines, upon which trains ran, was curiously fascinating, as was the whole business of ships and trains working harmoniously in such close proximity. Huge hemp ropes lay coiled upon the quayside as British Railways' cross-channel ships gently rose on the swell, nudging the pier and seemingly anxious to depart and steam hard away to France. A sudden deep loud blast from the ferry would make most people jump as the ship prepared to leave. With the wooden gangway taken away, the stayropes unleashed and the first dense clouds of smoke emitting from the funnel, the vessel moved ever more quickly as I tried to keep up with it by running along the pier. At the lighthouse we would watch it swing away and return a wave to those on board, who would be holding firmly onto hats and scarves. On windy days the stiff breeze blew straight in from the sea, sometimes sending spray splashing onto the pier which then drained away through little holes in the parapets back into the heaving, glossy-leaden sea-swell. The effects of continual drenching with salt water were only too apparent on the pier's ironwork where copious coats of paint attempted to halt the unrelenting march of flaking rust.

At the landward end of the pier the station buildings were rarely quiet, with people arriving for the next sailing, their suitcases being loaded onto large barrows. Green railway signs with perplexing wording in French, posters advertising romantic weekend breaks in Paris and trips to Holland, Germany, Switzerland and Italy added to the excitement and sense of adventure. Nearby, the noisy clatter of crockery and ringing of tills from the crowded buffet indicated another busy day for the women employed by the Southern Region's catering service. Idling outside, the locomotive crews took the opportunity to have one last 'cuppa' and enjoy a quick 'roll-up' before the departure of their train for the Junction. This was an occasion never to be missed and whilst attention was understandably drawn to the two or three engines at the front, the lone banking engine provided an equally heart-pounding spectacle, pushing for all its worth. The thought that fairly soon this common event would be no more never entered my mind, likewise that large passenger ferry ships would one day cease to sail from Folkestone. It all seemed so reassuringly immutable.

Following the closure of the Canterbury & Whitstable railway, further members of the 'R1' class became available. These mutilated engines, with their cut-down rounded cabs, stubby chimneys and boiler mountings for working the narrow Tyler Hill tunnel, looked especially odd. Their squat ugliness was worsened when coupled next to other 'R1's which had normal chimneys, domes and 'pagoda' cabs as rebuilt to Wainwright's elegant design. However, they were not strangers to the Folkestone Harbour branch since No. 1147 was often to be seen during the summer of 1950 creating a fine display of steam on the run up the incline. No. 1673, an LC&DR 'R' class 0-4-4T, was also used on the branch until being sent for scrap at the end of 1952, whilst another 'Chatham' engine, 'R1' No. 1708, was sometimes used around 1950, but apparently found little favour with the engine crews. Another very rare working seen banking was 'H' class 0-4-4T No. 31530, but yet again the tractive effort and performance of four-coupled wheeled locomotives as opposed to the old Stirling 0-6-0 arrangement on this very taxing steep climb to the Junction station left much to be desired.

Around 1955 Folkestone shed had seven survivors of the ex-SER 'R1' class, some being kept in store with generally only four in steam. These were, in their BR numbering: 31047, 31069, 31107, 31128, 31154, 31337 and 31340. When not employed shunting at the harbour, either on the quaysides or in the West Beach carriage sidings, they were often to be found at Folkestone Junction where, from the down platform, a good view could be obtained of the shed and turntable. Occasionally the 'R1's would be rostered for other duties such as moving empty coaching stock between the Central and Junction stations, shunting at Shorncliffe, as well as odd local workings through to Dover. The customary and cheerful 'cock-a-doodle-do', which echoed around the harbour from their unmistakeable South Eastern whistles, always made most people stop what they were doing and look up. Unwary visitors to Folkestone were quite spellbound as one - then two - then three tank engines began to venture forth from the Harbour station before rumbling over the swing bridge. While a chorus of safety valves blew in a deafening roar, great plumes of billowing white steam would be vented skywards from their chimneys, swirling round in vast clouds which followed the slowly-moving train. It seemed almost impossible that this pent-up steam could be safely contained within their boilers since their combined efforts were so plainly audible as to make them appear they were fit to burst. As the incline gradually stiffened so their exertion increased, sending great showers of sparks and smuts high into the air where startled herring gulls screeched and wheeled high above the fishmarket. Day-trippers to the town stood in awe alongside the cockle and whelk stalls with mouths agape, in wonderment at the spectacle unfolding before their eyes. The squealing of protesting carriage wheels was surpassed only by the echoing exhaust which resounded from the walls of nearby buildings as the trio reached their crescendo as the train continued up the Tram Road. Then, just as it seemed as if it was all over, a shout would often go up from someone: 'Look! - there's a fourth engine!' and pushing determinedly at the rear came another gallant 'R1'. These old Stirling tanks certainly gave every ounce of effort as heavy trains were hauled up this notorious incline. Sometimes it seemed as if they would not make it, their pace often slowing with extra-heavy trains, whilst the staccato being played on their combined exhausts sounding strained and faltering, but rarely did they ever fail their trusting crews.

The end for the faithful 'R1's finally came in the spring of 1959 when they were displaced by six ex-Great Western Railway 0-6-0 pannier tanks. Only 'R1's Nos. 31047 and 31337 lasted another year, retained by Folkestone Junction as

From the vicinity of 'Cliff Haven' a pair of Stirling tanks dissipating white steam across the Inner Harbour in the summer of 1958. In the background the SS Canterbury is seen starting away from the pier heading for Boulogne.

This gallant trio creating a spectacle heading across the inner harbour with the 2.25 p.m. Folkestone Harbour–Victoria service. The engines were 'R1' No. 1147 with cut-down cab and boiler mountings from its time spent working the Whitstable branch, another 'R1' No. 1107 and ex-LC&DR 'R' class 0–4–4T No. 1673. Banking at the rear was 'R1' No. 1337 depicted below. These pictures were taken on 12th October 1950.   J. J. SMITH

In their final days of operating the branch, 31337, 31174 and 31107 are seen here starting away from Platform 1 with the 1.10 p.m. boat train bound for Victoria on Saturday, 31st January 1959.

J. J. SMITH

Nos. 31128, 31107 and 31340 simmering in the warm afternoon sunshine at Folkestone Junction shed on 11th May 1952. Soon afterwards, the curved roof of the water tower was replaced with a new pitched roof. J. J. SMITH

No. 31174 along with another unidentified Stirling standing forlorn and disused in the old coaling road in April 1959 when they were displaced by the WR Pannier tanks. In the foreground was the 65ft turntable provided when the new 3-road shed was completed.
PETER WINDING

With steam to spare, one of the new British Railways 'Britannia' class, No. 70004 William Shakespeare, is seen speeding almost effortlessly through the Warren Halt with the 5.55 p.m. Dover Marine–Victoria 'Golden Arrow' service on Tuesday, 13th May 1952.

J. J. SMITH

WR Panniers Nos. 4630 and 4631 heading across the inner harbour with the Victoria-bound 'Golden Arrow' service on 20th June 1959. The nearby vendor on the whelk stall appears to have been enjoying a brisk trade as the warm summer weather settled into a memorable long spell.   J. J. SMITH

spare engines and for working ballast trains in connection with Phase Two of the Kent Coast electrification scheme. In spite of steam remaining the motive power for a further two years on the branch, it was never the same. For some reason the pannier tanks seemed utterly charmless, as well as looking distinctly out of place on the South Eastern. It was saddening to see the last two members of the gallant 'R1's lying idle at the back of Folkestone shed. Then one day, during the spring of 1960, I happened to be on the station platform at Shorncliffe as they came through on the local line, being hauled 'dead' to their last destination, the scrap road at Ashford.

Initially, the panniers suffered from priming and leaky tubes, thus their efficiency was distinctly impaired; on a few occasions they came to a stand near Folly Road crossing with insufficient steam. These problems were gradually overcome and the Folkestone men became used to these 'foreign' engines. According to Derek Cross: 'The panniers proved very popular on account of their good adhesion, but even so on anything like a heavy train, three or sometimes four had to be used'. However, come the day the panniers had to make way for electric traction, it seems no one mourned their passing.

The gradual displacement of steam traction from Folkestone's railways began around 1959 when diesel locomotives were used more often to haul the local services. These machines were considered far cleaner and more efficient, but there was no excitement or romance as far as I was concerned. Thankfully, most of the expresses, such as the midday 'Golden Arrow', were still left in charge of Bulleid's

Pacifics or sometimes a BR 'Britannia' class. The station platforms at Shorncliffe provided a good vantage point to see the 'Arrow' in full flight. Normally, a morning spent watching various trains come and go, as well as a 'C' class shunting the yard, was quite entertaining to a ten year-old, bored with 'train spotting' and pointlessly noting down numbers, preferring instead to simply soak up the atmosphere. Shortly after noon the bells in the signalbox would begin ringing out the coded messages, as the signalman would busy himself with his row of levers. I'd watch the line of semaphore signal arms bounce skywards, followed by the yellow distant arms below and know that the line had been made clear for the highlight of the morning. Looking towards Cheriton with the naked eye, it was possible to see as far as Horn Street, where the Elham Valley branch used to diverge. A dark shape with a trail of steam would appear, gradually growing in size as the familiar 'Golden Arrow' headboard became more distinct. Its speed was still fast enough to thrill as the distinctive beat of the Bulleid locomotives vibrated the ground, whilst the brakes were rarely applied until nearing Folkestone Central. In a few glorious moments the spectacle had dashed past on the through road, its sheer size, weight and power awesomely shaking the foundations of Shorncliffe. Jetting out smoke and steam which wafted across the platforms, the power from its exhaust and the heavy Pullman cars made it deafening in the extreme. The locomotive's name, emblazoned on the smooth casing sides, sometimes *Spitfire* or quite often *Hurricane*, complete with a large glinting arrow, added to the thrill. Following behind came those lovely cars with their romantic and mystical names:

An up boat train in the charge of 34014 rattling the teacups in the refreshment rooms of Shorncliffe station in July 1958. DEREK CROSS

Something to read on the train? Beneath the gas lights and glass canopies of the up side platform at Shorncliffe, Messrs. W. H. Smith & Son offered a variety of publications to pass away the time on the journey.

R. H. GREEN, CTY. PETER BAMFORD

Aquilla, Minerva, Phœnix, Orion, Hercules, Aries and *Pegasus* - all in a blur. As suddenly as it appeared, so was it all over, leaving just the roar from the swaying luggage vans, their wheels clattering over points and rail joints before fading into the distance, while the station signs remained swinging and creaking in the draught.

From my new school it was possible to see the railway embankment to the east of Shorncliffe station. The remaining steam-hauled locals would suddenly appear from behind the trees, whereupon I couldn't resist trying to see what was working the service - much to the exasperation of my French master. An annexe of the school was situated on Grace Hill where it was sometimes possible to sneak up to the roof at break times, even though it was strictly out of bounds. The flat roof provided a marvellous panorama of the old town, with the Foord viaduct in full view for a precious quarter of an hour. Sometimes, a wailing whistle would come during that most loathsome of times, a double period of physics. If engineered properly, I'd be able to position my feet on the rungs of the stool and elevate myself just enough to peer out of the high window behind to see what was making its way across the viaduct, before our tutor had finished writing on the board. Rarely was I caught out; even so, I can still remember the odd occasion when his strong Welsh accent which accompanied the stinging piece of well-aimed chalk as it clipped my ear: 'Hart - you are a *dreamer*, boy!'.

Alas, Monday, 12th June 1961, came all too quickly for some, but the hard work and planning put in by British Railways during the previous few years finally saw results. Folkestone Central station had been completely rebuilt with two sweeping island platforms, whilst modifications were made at Shorncliffe in readiness for the quadrupling of the railway from the Central station to Cheriton (Junction). The new electric trains which came gliding into Folkestone that day were greeted with a sense of pride and achievement, whilst the lordly 'Golden Arrow' was hauled by a new design of gleaming electric locomotion.

Whereas an undoubted advance came with electrification, there were no more friendly engine crews to whom I could wander up and meet. I remember how, as a very small boy in the early '50s, my parents had one day taken me up to the engine, where the kindly driver lifted me onto the footplate and showed me the controls. The firebox door was opened to reveal the awesome furnace, whilst the sight of brightly-burnished pipes and dials, the smell of coal, hot oil and steam deepened my fascination with railways. It was all a wonder and I was saddened when this particular link was finally broken.

The inexplicable aura which surrounded the dirty, everyday, steam locomotive could still be found for a while longer at Ashford. Here, on chilly Saturday mornings I'd find 'C' class 31690 shunting 'the hump', or one of the last class 'H' 0-4-4Ts, No. 31308, pottering around, but generally it was a woefully mournful place for there were so many locomotives lined-up awaiting scrapping. In the twilight of steam at Folkestone an Ashford 'C' class would regularly be

sent down to shunt the goods yard at Shorncliffe, a duty invariably performed by No. 31112. After school I'd forsake the warmth of home and the welcoming cup of tea and venture instead to Shorncliffe station where I'd hear the familiar rattling of trucks in the sidings. It was always very cold, the sun having already set in a clear and darkening winter sky with its pinkish horizon, the twinkling evening star and the promise of a sharp frost. Here I'd stand at the end of the platform, my feet numbed by the chill, but waiting patiently and faithfully to see old 31112. At around 4.40pm, its business finally over, it would clank out of the yard towards Cheriton before running down the line towards the signalbox in order to gain the 'up' road. To a 12 year-old mind it resembled a little farewell, almost like coming down to see me before running back light to Ashford, so there I'd watch it disappear, my teeth chattering and eyes watering in the biting wind. Into the dusky gloom it went, my ears straining to hear the fading steady beat, but not until the tail lights became indistinguishable did I turn and head for home and its warm welcome. One dismal evening, 31112 was not there and failed to turn up ever again. I read later that it had been reallocated to Faversham shed for snow plough duty, after which it had been despatched to Ashford works in the spring of 1962 for scrapping. It was only a machine composed of iron, steel, brass and copper. Nevertheless, I felt a sense of loss and it is perhaps remarkable that, forty years later, I can still recall those vivid images as though it were only yesterday.

My after-school trips to Shorncliffe became less frequent although I still enjoyed talking to the remaining staff and soaking up the ambience of this once-grand and lovely station. A blazing fire always greeted me in the down side booking hall where a cast-iron fender still defiantly bore the legend 'SE&CR', while above, gas lights hissed and 'popped', their yellowish light far cosier than electric bulbs.

Over the weekend 17th/18th February 1962 the new colour light signalling was brought into use. Shorncliffe signalbox was quickly demolished that night, whilst the original station building of 1863, which had survived for so long as a goods office, had been similarly swept away a few months earlier. The new 'up' platform was then extended and

The last days of Shorncliffe signal box with its friendly staff.

the quadrupling finished. At Folkestone Junction a new panel box was opened to control movements between Ashford and Archcliffe Junction at Dover. Shorncliffe lost its gas lamps, the lovely glass, cast-iron and decorative wooden canopies along the approach road sides were removed, whilst the glorious stained glass windows, some of which had been presented by Canadian troops during the Great War, were taken out and given away or sold. The refreshment facilities on the 'up' side also went, the dusty room locked and deserted, no longer providing the cheerful welcome I so fondly remembered.

Steam returned to Folkestone in February 1962 with 'The Kentish Venturer', a rail tour organized by the Locomotive Club of Great Britain. The honour fell to 'King Arthur' class, No. 30782, perhaps appropriately for me, *Sir Brian*. Eagerly I looked forward to seeing it steaming along the embankment from the viaduct, then through the Central station before arriving at Shorncliffe where there was a scheduled stop. On that Sunday, *Sir Brian* performed well, delighting the many railway enthusiasts and sightseers who clambered everywhere to secure a snapshot. However, I couldn't understand why it didn't feel the same as those wistful recollections from my receding boyhood.

The long, severe winter of 1962/3 provided me with yet another unforgettable memory when two of the last three 'C' class locomotives, Nos. 31592 and 31271, turned up with snowploughs to clear the blocked lines of East Kent. I watched this pair of grimy, unkempt, Edwardian engines drift along the 'up' local line from Shorncliffe station and into Cheriton cutting where a colour-light signal brought them to a stand. There they paused, white steam blasting deafeningly from their safety valves as, for a few precious minutes, the thrill and excitement I'd once known came flooding back. With a green aspect, they creaked into motion, sending huge plumes of white dissipating steam into the cold grey skies which relentlessly cloaked Kent during that long winter. I waited as they disappeared into the distance for Ashford where I later read they'd had a run down the New Romney branch.

In September 1962 Shorncliffe was renamed Folkestone West, whilst the Junction became Folkestone East, a seemingly pointless exercise in view of the fact that the latter station was closed only three years later. The staffing at Shorncliffe was further reduced, familiar faces disappeared and there was even less of interest as these years rolled by and the modernization and rationalization of British Railways took place.

Changes throughout the ensuing decade, up until 1980, were relatively minor. The size of the station buildings at Shorncliffe was quite drastically reduced during the spring of 1979 when more than a third at the London end was demolished. At the Junction station all the buildings, dating from 1844, were completely removed soon after closure, whilst an air of desolation quickly developed where at one time there had been so much frantic activity. Nevertheless, reminders of the past survived for many years later, such as

the gates to the former yard bearing plates marked 'SE&CR'. Today, though, new road schemes and houses cover much of the former station and railway yards.

Every trace of the old Central station was swept away with the rebuilding programme of 1959, but perhaps those who find the unfriendly gaunt architecture of the 1960s interesting will not be disappointed. Whilst the optimism and confidence of that era still pervades its windswept platforms and draughty, vaulted concrete passageways which resemble the entrance to an Egyptian tomb, no one could possibly care to linger here. The need for quadruple lines between here and Cheriton disappeared with the opening of the Channel Tunnel and the loss of the boat trains to Folkestone and Dover. The fast lines which once carried such expresses as the 'Golden Arrow' and the 'Night Ferry' eventually grew weeds, turned rusty and were finally lifted in the mid-1990s, a sight no one would have thought possible three decades earlier on the day when BR's chairman, Dr. Richard Beeching, proudly visited the smart new station. Further changes were to follow when, in 1998, the 'up' London line was slewed across to make use of the former 'down' fast platform face. This enabled economies to be effected whereby the 'up' island platform became redundant, along with its steel and glass canopies, vaulted subway, waiting rooms and buffet which have all since been razed.

Folkestone Harbour, at the time of writing, clings on to a past that seems ever more threatened, but for the time being there remain vestiges of a lost age. Along the pleasant cobbled Stade, fishermen still land their catches of fish, crabs, shrimps and cockles, providing a suitable cameo of seaside life for today's eager visitors. Embedded along a portion of its length remain some of the long-disused rails leading to the former SE&CR workshops and ship repair yard, whilst behind 'The Cabin' café linger traces of an old SER wagon turntable. These artefacts invariably cause more inquisitive passers-by to pause and wonder.

Surprisingly, the Harbour branch has managed to survive for well over a hundred and fifty years, but its future seems far from secure and closure appears possible. Nevertheless, the history of Folkestone's railways continues to evolve. Who, two decades ago, could have confidently predicted that railway lines would soon convey trains beneath the noble hill, where popular folklore holds that mighty Cæsar camped, then onwards under the English Channel? Now, in the small hours of night, my parents hear trains running over these new lines, through the enchanting lost meadows, woodlands, hayfields and clay ponds where I wandered aimlessly and played so blissfully for hours as a boy.

Thus, Sir Edward Watkin's long-cherished dream of a railway linking Britain with the rest of Europe has finally come true, a century after his great aspirations, but what might the next hundred years have in store? Will we soon witness the abandonment of the branch down the old Tram Road, accompanied by the entire redevelopment of the harbour as anticipated by speculative developers? Could the combined forces of nature and climate change once more reshape the Warren on such a catastrophic scale as to render the railway unworthy of rebuilding?

It is to be hoped that the value of railways will be appreciated by politicians. Railways are indispensable and still represent economic health and well-being to those parts of the country where they have been retained. Our choked and polluted island will need them even more in the future and the trust placed in them by our Victorian predecessors was not misguided, but has subsequently been simply abused. A British invention it may have been, yet we may only marvel how our continental neighbours have financed and

developed their railways. Thankfully, Folkestone has been more fortunate than many other towns for the benefits of rail travel are still available to its residents and must be vigilantly safeguarded.

Perhaps the shepherd who grazed his flock of sheep in Foord meadows more than a hundred and sixty years ago wondered what his rural landscape would look like in the future. Unquestionably, the coming of the railway instigated and moulded modern Folkestone, enabling the growth of a lovely town with a rich, varied and absorbing history. This, I'm certain, is not the end of the story, but merely the closing of a chapter.

DAVID LAWRENCE

A Stirling 'R' class with a good head of steam approaching East Cliff crossing on its way to the Junction station in June 1907. The elegance of the three-arch span of Radnor bridge may be appreciated whilst, judging by the 'out of use' crosses on the distant arms, the tall bracketed SER signal of Saxby & Farmer origin had just been replaced. COLLECTION R. C. RILEY

ACKNOWLEDGEMENTS

In my desire to present the best possible illustrations, I have been extremely fortunate in having the kind assistance of so many local historians and photographers.

To say that this book would be considerably poorer were it not for the co-operation of my good friend Alan Taylor is abundantly no exaggeration to anyone glancing at the credits to the illustrations. As a result I feel overwhelmed by his kindness and feel I cannot sufficiently express my thanks and gratitude for his wonderful contribution. Alan's interest in old Folkestone is well-known in the area and is to his immense credit, especially for the diligence he has shown in his own publications, as well as his dedicated efforts to conserve the town's archive. I would also like to thank my other friends associated with Folkestone's marvellous Local History Society, Peter Bamford and Eamonn Rooney for their assistance during the compilation of this book and their willingness to be of help.

Among my 'railway friends' I feel a great debt to 'J. J.' – John Smith, whose seemingly untiring sojourns across the country with a camera to record the last decades of steam have allowed us to glimpse so much of what has entirely disappeared. Always modest about his accomplishments, I never fail to be impressed by John's skillful camerawork. Denis Cullum and Dick Riley have also displayed great kindness in helping me out, as has James Aston, Reg Randell, Richard Cullen, Roger Carpenter and not least Richard Casserley on behalf of his father 'H. C.' – one of the 'legends' in railway photography.

Sadly, I must give posthumous thanks to the Reverend Mace, with whom I corresponded, also to Rita and George Stickler, who showed me such kind hospitality on my visits to their home at Blean.

My sincere thanks are extended to Tonbridge Historical Society, similarly the staff at the excellent Heritage Room at Folkestone Library, which is a great credit to the town. Equally, I should like to express my gratitude to those wonderful institutions, the British Newspaper Library and the Public Record Office at Kew. The same applies to all the numerous staff I have been acquainted with over the years formerly employed by the Southern Region of British Railways.

Finally, enduring gratitude goes to Paul, June and Ann at Wild Swan Publications for 'working the magic' and producing such a truly handsome book.